FUN AND AMAZING FACTS FOR KIDS

A Fascinating Book of Information for Curious Kids

by RONNY the FRENCHIE

Bonus!

Dear parents,

I am thrilled to have your child join me on this exciting fact-finding journey! But guess what? There's even more to explore!

Join me once again and dive into the captivating stories of extraordinary sport heroes and fearless entrepreneurs. I can't wait to share their remarkable tales of innovation and determination with you. In addition to the inspiring stories, I have included some fantastic coloring pages that will spark your children's creativity too!

So, what are you waiting for? Claim the freebies by scanning the QR code below or type riccagarden.com/ronny_freebies into your web browser.

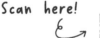

Your Frenchie,

RONNY

Note: You must be 16 years or older to sign up, so grab your parent for help if you need to.

Contents

Welcome!

Hello kids, Ronny the Frenchie, your favorite bulldog, here!

Are you ready to set off on a super-duper journey of learning about the most exciting and interesting things in the world and universe?

There's a lot to discover when you've got your nose to the ground, and I should know—my nose is always sniffing out new and interesting facts (and maybe a buried bone or two)!

I've been around the world collecting all sorts of fun and interesting facts to include in this amazing book because I know how much kids love to learn about the world they live in.

But, shh... Let me tell you a little secret first.

I used to be just your ordinary everyday sleep-all-day and slobber a lot type of bulldog; you know what I mean—waiting for my meals, someone to scratch the back of my ear, and my daily walks through pretty Paris.

Life was simple and good until the day I climbed to the top

of the Eiffel Tower during a thunderstorm and got hit right between my eyes by a bolt of thunder! But don't worry! I didn't get hurt—oh no, something far more marvelous happened.

My brain suddenly grew a whole two inches, and actually started to work, demanding more food, aka knowledge. Although I still love regular food too!

So I stopped sniffing around for buried bones and started sniffing out facts to feed my hungry brain. And I found so many interesting, exciting, amazing, stupendous, scary, and impressive facts (phew, that left me breathless!), that I had to put them all together in one super-duper book for you to read. Oh, and by the way, I love regular food too, especially bananas!

"Ooh, want to hear a banana joke?"

When I'm leaving the house, what do I say to the bananas in my kitchen?

I am going bananas!

My second favorite thing to do, apart from eating bananas, of course, is exploring. I've enjoyed adventures along the mysterious Amazon River where a piranha once nipped my tail and trekked to the summit of Mount Everest where I almost froze my nose off. They are among some of the exciting adventures I will never forget.

You won't believe how fascinating our world and universe are. There is so much to learn about; for example, did you know that every time you tell a lie—your nose actually gets warmer (not longer, mind you)? This phenomenon is called the "Pinocchio Effect." How weird is that?

This fact was discovered through a study conducted by the University of Granada's Department of Experimental Psychology. The discovery was made through a 'thermography,' which is a device to measure body temperature (*Pinocchio Effect*, 2012).

So, the next time you decide to tell your mom a fib, you better make sure she doesn't touch your nose! Mine is always cold as a sign of my good health, and also as an indication of what a good little bulldog I am.

If you found that fact fascinating, you will certainly love the information I have included in each chapter covering all your favorite subjects from science to sports and much more.

Now don't worry, this isn't your typical boring old book.! I know how much you guys like to learn about fun and unique topics. Therefore, I have added plenty of mind-boggling facts to keep you from falling asleep while reading my book. Which you won't!

Chapter 1: Science & Technology

I must agree that science and technology are fascinating subjects. And, no—that does not make me a nerd!

Okay, so you never expected a bulldog to agree that everything is related to math! But since I am no ordinary bulldog, I know better. And so will you. Check out these amazing facts about math.

AMAZING AND COOL FACTS ABOUT MATH

Okay, so are you getting suspicious about me using the words 'cool' and 'math' in the same sentence? Let me show you that math really can be cool, and loving the subject makes you more than a nerd. It makes you super smart and ready to face any challenge.

Totally Fun and Cool Math Facts

The letter 'A' is used in only one number when spelling numbers out from zero to thousand

Can you guess which number that is?

> Answer: Thousand—none of the other numbers before thousand are spelled using the letter 'A.'

If you already knew that, give your tail a wag! Oops, I forgot you probably don't have a tail. In that case, give yourself a pat on the back!

Roman numerals do not have a zero. Have you ever noticed?

Roman numerals start from the number one (I) and have no zero. Here are some fun facts surrounding the concept of zero.

The ancient Romans only used their numerals for trade in order to know how much and how many goods they were trading for and with. Therefore, they found no need for a zero to be a part of their numerics.

The Romans also found this convenient as they did not have to keep a column-free in the accounts book for a zero. Instead, they used the word 'nulla' to indicate 'nothingness' (*nulla* means nothing in Latin). Don't you love that word? Nothingness!

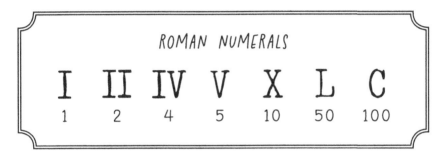

ROMAN NUMERALS

I	II	IV	V	X	L	C
1	2	4	5	10	50	100

Also, as you know, they had no calculators and used a contraption called an abacus, also called a counting frame, for their mathematical needs. The abacus also had no column for zero.

The ancient Greeks did have an understanding of zero, as in "there are no oranges," but saw no use for a symbol to represent the concept. The great Aristotle (who I can only assume was a dog lover) decided that there really was no need for zero as you could not divide a number by zero and arrive at a substantial result. For example, you cannot add zero bones to zero bones and feed a hungry dog.

The first zero appeared in an abacus around 1,500 years ago in India when a dot was used to symbolize a zero in an abacus. That dot grew and expanded into the '0' we all know today.

By about the 8th century, the zero started to get noticed and caught the interest of an Arab known as al-Khwarizmi, who was a mathematician and a traveler. He decided it was time to introduce Mr. '0' to Europe as part of the standard Arabic numerics we all use today (you know, 1, 2, 3, 4, and so on).

At first Mr. '0' was not a huge hit in Europe; the Italians were quite suspicious and did not like a zero barging in on their traditional numerical system. Poor Mr. '0' was branded as "not needed," and a law was passed in the year 1299, banning the use of the numeric zero or any of the newly-arrived Arabic numerals in any documents or contracts in Italy (boy, they really loved their Roman numerals). And so, to this day, Roman numerals do not have a zero.

ITALY

Although Arabic numerals are the most widely used numerics across the globe, Roman numerals are still used to indicate book chapters, to keep track of the National Football League's Super Bowls, to mark the hours on the face of a clock, in chemistry, and for indicating the winter and summer Olympic titles. Now aren't those cool facts?

A pie chart is called a Camembert

Camembert is a lovely soft French cheese, but in France, it is not only a cheese. In my home country, Camembert also refers to a pie chart or circle graph. Because we Frenchies love our cheese, a pie chart reminds us of our creamy Camembert cheese rounds. And so when in France, if you are asked to draw Camembert, make sure you know which type.

Interesting fact on pie charts

 The round pie chart with wedges to represent values seems to make most societies across the world think of food. Therefore, a simple pie chart goes by many delicious names (ooh, I'm getting hungry!).

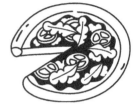

In China, a pie chart is often referred to as a flatbread or a round cookie chart.

In Portugal and Brazil, it's even called a pizza chart.

 And the best name for a pie chart comes from several countries (Germany, Turkey, Italy, Sweden, Norway) who refer to it as a cake diagram. I would call it a banana pie.

Obelus

Do you know what an obelus is? It's the name of the division symbol (÷). This symbol (obelus) was first used to represent division in math in the year 1659. It was introduced in an algebra book called *Teutsche Algebra* written by Johann Rahn, a Swiss mathematician. Johann is also the person who introduced this symbol ∴ which means 'therefore.'

Mathematical symbols didn't exist before the 14 - 16th centuries

That's right kiddos, there were no symbols to indicate addition, subtraction, division, and much more until around the 14th to 16th centuries. Instead, people used words to indicate the equations.

For example, teachers probably wrote "add 12 to 22" or "100 divided by 10 equals 10." It took people longer to write the question than it did to find the solution. Therefore, just as Johann Rahn invented the math version of the obelus to mean, other mathematicians invented mathematical symbols over time. How many mathematicians do you know who invented math symbols?

A jiffy is an actual unit of time

I met this really smart mathematician in Egypt while I was there following the scent of some really delicious smelling-bones inside a pyramid. When I told him I wanted to go check out the Sphinx and would be back in a jiffy, he scoffed and said the Sphinx is much too far for me to be back within a jiffy. Because, you see, a jiffy actually refers to a unit of time: 1/100 of a second to be precise. Goodness, and all along I thought it was just a term we used to mean quick!

Computer animation uses the term jiffy to define playback time, which is 1/100 of a second. Therefore, the time frame is measured in jiffies. Jiffies are used as units of time for electronics and in physics as well.

So, the next time your mom asks you to be back in a jiffy, make sure to ask for more time—unless you have superpowers!

Superstitious number thirteen

When writing the words "eleven plus two" and "twelve plus one," there are exactly thirteen letters! Whoa! Not only do the actual numbers (11

+ 2 and 12 + 1) add up to 13, but there are 13 letters used to write out the equations themselves. That's a pretty awesome fact if you ask me, and cool trivia to impress your friends with. Thirteen is also a superstitious number as it has biblical significance. For example, there were 13 people at the last supper before Jesus was betrayed, and throughout time, 13 has been associated with bad luck. Some hotels don't even have a room numbered 13 and some even skip numbering an entire floor the 13th, instead going from the 12th floor right to the 14th floor.

 I'm in the mood for some banana pie right now, so let's take a break! It's trivia time kids.

Math Trivia

1. Who invented the paint-by-number system?

2. In which year was the equal (=) symbol invented?

3. Who holds the Guinness Book of Records record for being the fastest human calculator?

4. In recorded history, where were the very first math games played?

5. There is only one even prime number, what is it?

6. The Roman numeral X equals what number?

7. What number does not have a matching Roman numeral?

8. What number is considered to be lucky by most people?

9. How many loaves of bread would you get if you ordered a baker's dozen?

The answers are on the next page!

Answers

1. Who invented the paint-by-number system?

Leonardo da Vinci. He used the paint-by-number system to teach his students and apprentices the basics in choosing appropriate colors for various types of painting.

He would hand out patterns with numbers indicating which color to use where.

2. In which year was the equal (=) symbol invented?

1557 by Robert Recorde

3. Who holds the Guinness Book of Records record for being the fastest human calculator?

Scott Flansburg of Phoenix, Arizona, won the record for fastest human calculator on April 27th, 2000. Since then, there have been many who claim to be the fastest human calculator, but Scott's feat is the only one recorded thus far.

4. In recorded history, where were the very first math games played?

In Africa, where they played mancala.

Did you know that mancala happens to be one of the oldest games in the world, and quite possibly one of the oldest math games? The origins of mancala can be traced back to an archaeological site called Matara in Eritrea, as well as Yeha in Ethiopia, where the game originated around 700 A.D.

5. There is only one even prime number, what is it?

Two

6. The Roman numeral X equals what number?

Ten

7. What number does not have a matching Roman numeral?

Zero of course

8. What number is considered to be lucky by most people?

Lucky number seven (Bonus: because seven often represents perfection)

9. How many loaves of bread would you get if you ordered a baker's dozen?

Thirteen. In Medieval times, bakers who sold underweight bread were punished badly, and so to avoid any punishments such as severe flogging, bakers always added an extra loaf to their dozen.

Famous Mathematicians Who Helped Change Our World

Numero uno, Ronny the Frenchie! Haha no, that's just a joke kids, although with my super brain I could be one.

WHO IS A MATHEMATICIAN?

Any person who makes use of math in their daily work to figure out stuff.

Even you and I are mathematicians at different times; when we are using math to solve problems or figure out certain things. That's right, so we are all cool math cats!

Math is one of the coolest subjects around, and without it, we would be in quite a bit of trouble. Think about it—without math, you would not even have a home because your parents would not have a way of calculating their incomes and purchasing a house, car, groceries—or even dog food!

You, too, can become a whiz at math just like these famous mathematicians who helped us figure out many problems, theories, and formulas. Did you know that without the help of some top mathematicians, some of whom I have listed below, there would be no scientists? And no Tony Stark doing all those rad calculations on his virtual screen to invent the latest Iron Man suit?!

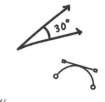

That's right—math played a HUGE role in changing how our world progressed, and we owe it all to the following people who took math to new heights.

Charles Babbage

Charles Babbage is considered the "father of computers" because he is credited with presenting plans for the world's very first Mechanical Computing Device. A mathematician and skilled inventor from England (where they have delicious bangers and mash that I love to eat), Charles

Babbage could not complete his work because of a lack of funds. But his theories and proposals certainly sparked a newfound interest in the field of computing science for which we are all thankful today.

Countess Ada Lovelace

Now here is a great lady I would love to know. Ada Lovelace was the daughter of the famous English poet Lord Byron. She was one of the smartest women in England and worked with Charles Babbage. Calling herself an analyst, Countess Ada helped

Babbage build his analytical engines and was the world's very first computer programmer—how cool is that?!

Babbage respected Ada's intelligence so much that he called her "Enchantress of Numbers." Sadly, the lovely countess died at the age of 36, but her important notes on programming helped us to come up with the very first computer program.

$$ax^2 + by^2 + c = 0$$

Sir Isaac Newton

Hey kids, I know it's still too early, but at some point, you are going to wonder who invented calculus. Well, it was this guy, Sir Isaac Newton.

But did you know that Sir Newton is credited with inventing more than calculus?

He introduced the world to early physics where he made people take a closer look at the universe, as well as developing theories on motion and gravity.

The theory of gravitational power. We all know the story about the apple falling from the tree and Sir Isaac discovering gravity. Well, no one knows for sure if the story is true, but Sir Isaac sure did discover the theory of gravity and went on to explain a universal force that causes particles at rest to move between point A and point B.

The scientific method can help turn theories into facts. Newton used observations, calculations, and the results from certain phenomena to prove a theory with evidence to back it up, instead of merely theorizing.

Blaise Pascal

The inventor of the very first mechanical calculator, this very smart Frenchman from my own beloved France was a great inventor and mathematician. Renowned in the 17th century, Pascal was also a physicist and is credited with finalizing the theory of Pressure and Vacuum, the roulette wheel, and inventing the syringe (I'm not sure I'm too fond of this invention because I dislike getting my shots at the vet).

Theodore von Kármán

Born in Budapest, Theodore von Kármán left his motherland to come to the United States and work for CalTech. He helped launch Aerojet, which was one of America's largest rocket and missile propulsion companies.

Kármán was also responsible for putting forward the theory behind supersonic flights and is even credited with the earliest design of the helicopter. He also helped found the aeronautic research group for North Atlantic Treaty Organization (NATO).

Amazing Space Facts

Space is still very much a mystery to our brilliant scientists, and we still have so much more to learn about the solar system, far-away galaxies, planets, and stars. However, there are a lot of cool and amazing facts about space that we do know. And so, I visited NASA to learn more cool space facts you may be interested in checking out.

Did You Know? Space Facts

The sun is a million times larger than the Earth

This means that we could fit a million of our Earths inside the enormous sun. However, we could not get near enough to try it because the sun is very, very hot. According to NASA, its core is 27 million °F (15 million °C) while the surface can be less at around 10,000 °F.

On mars, you would see a blue sunset!

NASA tells us that a Martian sunset would appear blue. The reason is the fine dust found in the atmosphere which helps blue light to infiltrate the atmosphere more easily than other colors.

NASA actually has a picture posted of a Red Planet (aka, Mars) sunset, which is more of a muted blue due to reduced dust particles in the atmosphere on the day the picture was taken. Search online for NASA pictures of Mars sunset to see this pretty phenomenon.

A day on Venus is almost a year on Earth

If you waited one day to celebrate your birthday on Venus, you would actually miss close to a whole year of your life! Even more for me because one dog year is equal to fifteen human years.

A normal day consisting of daytime and nighttime is called a "solar day."

On our beautiful planet Earth, a solar day is 24 hours, or one day.

On Venus, a solar day is 5,832 hours which is about 243 Earth days, or almost eight months on Earth.

I will not be visiting Venus anytime soon, because I don't want to return as Ronny the Grandpa Frenchie!

Cool facts about Saturn's rings!

Are Saturn's ring revolving razor blades put there to chop up approaching enemy spaceships? Nope, they are not, but I like to think so.

In reality, Saturn's rings are made up of different particles. NASA knows this because they have now sent a total of four robotic spacecraft up to check out what the deal is with Saturn's ring. Those spacecrafts are:

PIONEER 2   VOYAGER I   VOYAGER II   CASSINI

Here are some facts they revealed about Saturn's rings

There are around 500–1000 rings encircling Saturn.

The rings are 240,000 miles wide, which is almost the distance from our planet Earth to the moon, 238,855 miles. However, the rings are not very fat at only 100 miles in thickness.

Each of Saturn's rings is made up of particles. Some are humongous, about the size of your school bus, while others are smaller than an ant and cannot be seen with the naked eye.

Just like in the movies, there are gaps between the rings.

The Cassini spacecraft spent the most time exploring Saturn's rings. Launched in 1997, it got there in 2004, after a seven-year journey, and spent a total of 13 years helping scientists at NASA learn more about Saturn's ring, its moons, and atmosphere.

Inside the Cassini spacecraft, scientists sent along a probe. It was called Huygens (pronounced Hoy-guns). The probe was sent into the atmosphere of Saturn's largest moon, which scientists named Titan. The pictures Huygens sent back were amazing and helped scientists at NASA learn more about Saturn.

On September 15th, 2017, Cassini carried out its final mission and dove into the upper atmosphere of Saturn. It was a planned maneuver to help NASA learn more about the planet's surface, which they have never seen. The spacecraft continuously sent data back to Earth as it plummeted down to Saturn's surface. Midway through its descent, it broke apart and became part of the planet it had been exploring for the last 20 years. (Sorry, I need a minute to dry my tears. Bye bye, Cassini, thanks for the memories!).

Space junk is created by us

Also called space debris, space junk consists of leftover bits of satellites, broken pieces from rocket ship launches, bits of paint that peel off rockets, and even a dropped spanner or two from when astronauts were trying to repair space stations or satellites.

From as far back as the 1950s, we have been launching satellites and rocket ships into space, and the remaining junk from dead machines and parts is starting to pose a threat as scientists believe the probability of recently-launched spaceships crashing into space debris is growing very high.

As of June 1, 2021, there are over 6,542 satellites that are orbiting Earth at the moment. Of these, 3,372 are active satellites, while 3,172 are dead satellites (*How many satellites*, 2022).

If we were to fly a rocket to space, we would have to watch out for those 3,172 dead satellites, as well as other space debris that could come hurtling toward us at any moment!

The world's first satellite

The world's first satellite to be launched was Sputnik.

The Soviet Union launched Sputnik at 19:28:34 UTC on October 4, 1957. It was a great achievement for mankind and space exploration.

Sputnik was built as a shiny metal sphere, and it resembled a basketball in size weighing a total of 183.9 pounds (83.6 kg).

Sputnik was launched into space on an enormous rocket ship.

It orbited the Earth for three weeks, traveling a total distance of 43.5 million miles around our planet. Sputnik lasted for three months before its batteries died and it finally fell out of orbit and crashed through Earth's atmosphere.

There was a tiny radio transmitter inside Sputnik which sent a beeping sound to Earth, and people all over the world could listen to that sound over the radio.

Sputnik was meant to mean "fellow traveler," although in Russia, 'Sputnik' is now colloquial for 'satellite.'

The birth of NASA

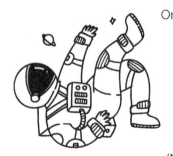

Once Sputnik was launched, the US decided it was time to get into the space game. Exactly one year after the launch of the world's first satellite by the USSR, US President Dwight Eisenhower established the National Aeronautics and Space Administration (NASA). This was the formal launch of what is called the "space race" between the US and Russia.

The launch of NASA and the space race saw both the US and Russia make great strides in space exploration, leading to the first moon landing by the US in 1969.

The first moon landing

On July 20th, 1969 the first spaceship carrying astronauts orbited the moon. Apollo 11 blasted off to space carrying onboard astronauts Neil Armstrong, Buzz Aldrin, and Michael Collins.

Neil Armstrong and Buzz Aldrin got in the lunar module, called Eagle, and descended to the moon. Michael Collins remained within Columbus, the main command module, which is the breakaway part from Apollo 11.

The Eagle landed on the part of the moon called the Sea of Tranquility. It was then that Armstrong said the famous words, "The Eagle has landed!"

Neil Armstrong is the first man to set foot on the moon, followed by Buzz Aldrin. NASA heard the following from Armstrong: *"That's one small step for a man, one giant leap for mankind"* (*July 20, 1969*, 2019).

If you leave a footprint on the moon, it will be there for a million years

According to NASA, footprints on the moon last almost forever because the moon has no atmosphere. There is no wind or water flow to erase footprints, and so there is nothing to erase them.

A dog was the first living being sent to space

That's right kids, we dogs can make history too! Laika, a Russian dog, was the first living creature sent to space on November 3, 1957. A street dog, Laika was selected and trained for her space journey. She was a very brave dog, despite showing signs of anxiety and fear. Laika blasted off to space on Sputnik 2. Sadly, the rocket crashed on Earth, but Laika lives on forever as the first living being sent to space.

INTERESTING TECH FACTS

There are many exciting topics when it comes to technology, and each one is mind-blowing in its own way. Prepare to be amazed at the amount of information I was able to gather on my adventures. Our world is constantly evolving and changing with many geniuses inventing new technology to make our lives easier and more interesting. Although, I must confess, nothing beats a good early-morning run in the park and playing frisbee with my human friend.

Check out these cool tech facts and see which one is most interesting to you! Maybe you will become a great inventor too! I am looking for an extraordinary mechanic to help me maintain my time machine which I use to learn more about the past. More on that later though. Now let's look at some totally terrific tech facts!

Fiber Optics - The Backbone of All Modern Communication Infrastructure

This is the most widely-used and fastest technology for sending information across the internet. Fiber optics replace copper cables as they are faster, offer clearer, sharper images, and are of a higher quality overall.

Optical fibers are as thin as one strand of hair and are made from a mix of plastic, silica glass, or both. A bunch of the fibers gets twisted together to form a cable, quite like when you take a bunch of your hair and twist it up.

The thin fiber hairs encased in an outer cover are called the core of a fiber optic cable and send data in the form of light.

Now, you know how fast light travels, right kids?

Well, fiber optics uses light to send information super fast from one place to another. The data is transformed into light by a transmitter and travels through the cable so fast that it can reach long distances in nanoseconds. Fiber optics are used in telephones and computer cables.

Doctors use them when they want to see what's going on inside your body. A device called an 'endoscope,' made up of a bunch of optical fibers, helps doctors see inside your body because some of those fibers reflect light and illuminate the insides of the body, and some can carry back images for the doctor to see.

An endoscopy test is how doctors found out where the key I accidentally swallowed was sitting in my tummy. Safe to say I pooped it out in two days—gross, yes I know!

The first optical phone was invented by Alexander Graham Bell in the 1880s, but it wasn't until the 1970s that fiber optics were first used for the telephone to transfer data.

More interesting facts on fiber optics and light!

The concept of using light to transmit data was first conceived by two French inventors way back in the 1840s. Their names were Jacques Babinet and Daniel Colladon. They showed how light could be guided to travel long distances through refraction. Wow! We French are really smart!

Once the concept of refracting light to travel long distances was established, scientists found new ways to manipulate and use light for the transfer of data.

In 1850, John Tyndall, a very smart inventor from Ireland, did an experiment to show how light could travel through water fountains.

His demonstrations were so inspiring that another very smart inventor and scientist from nearby Scotland—John Logie Baird—went on to develop the world's very first television.

Logie Baird held a demonstration and transmitted images that, to everyone's amazement, moved! This very first demonstration of a working television was done at the London Institute in 1925. Mind how far television has come since its humble beginnings! Now you know how long it took for technicians to perfect the television and offer us Smart TVs—who knows what's next!

John Tyndall and his experiment with light and water fountains inspired another very smart scientist, Narinder Singh Kapany who, in 1952, invented the very first fiber optical cable in England.

By the 1990s, with the growing popularity of the internet, fiber optic cables were further advanced and laid out across the world, connecting us all through its light refraction transmissions—isn't that just awesome?

Because of a simple concept thought up in the 1840s, I can now order my favorite banana pie online with the click of a button. Oops, that's the doorbell kids, time to collect my afternoon tea!

Quick Cell Phone Facts

We all know what a mobile phone is; also called a cell phone, or handphone, and now more popularly, a smartphone. Your parents have them, your brothers and sisters have them, and maybe even you own one.

I have my very own paw phone.

I've got the latest version because a curious bulldog like me needs to stay connected. And that is just what a cell phone does—keeps you connected, plus so MUCH more.

Mobile phones: Did you know?

A portable telephone capable of sending and receiving calls as well as text messages is called a cellular phone, or cell phone.

The first portable phone was called a 'cellular' phone because areas that received the radio

signals emitted by the first mobile phones were separated into areas that were called cells.

A smartphone serves the same function as a cell phone, but has many more capabilities as it is also a mini-computer able to perform a variety of tasks—such as playing Minecraft, my favorite game!

The world's first cell phone

Martin Cooper invented the world's first cell phone on April 3rd, 1973. He made the first call to Joel S. Engel, who was his nemesis and worked at Bell Labs—yup, you guessed it, Joel was the competition, and Cooper called to let him know about his amazing invention.

The very first cell phone was sold to the public in 1983. It was the Motorola DynaTAC 8000x, which was almost the size of a brick and certainly did not fit in anyone's pocket, but it could be carried around and was mobile. So people loved it as a sort of status symbol.

This phone was in fact nicknamed "the brick," and it was heavy to carry around, weighing about two pounds. And best, or maybe worst, of all, the battery lasted only for 30 minutes—which made  the price tag of $3,995 USD seem too high for many people to invest in a mobile phone that only lasted for half an hour.

Smartphone Facts

The very first smartphone to be invented was called the Simon Personal Communicator (SPC). It offered some of the basic features seen in modern smartphones that you and I love to watch YouTube on. Invented in 1992 by a company called IBM, the SPC phone had a touch screen you could use with the aid of a stylus. The battery lasted for a whole hour.

 The very first Apple iPhone was introduced to the world by Steve Jobs in 2007. He unveiled his creation at the Macworld Convention. The superior phone had a range of features everyone loved. Camera, touch screen, iPod, plus it was the first mobile phone that offered internet capabilities—yay!

In this very first iPhone, Jobs introduced what he called a "killer app." Do you know what it was? Simple; it was taking calls. No other phone offered an easier way to make a call than the Apple iPhone. You see kids before the smartphone came along, we had buttons to press on a mobile phone to make a call. We could not simply search for a number and touch the screen for it to dial; the phone number had to be manually punched in, and bummer if you accidentally pressed the wrong button. Ask your parents about dialing numbers on phones before the smartphone came along.

The best part of that unveiling was when Steve Jobs called Starbucks. I was there, you know, gaping in awe as he opened the app for Google Maps, found Starbucks, and called the place right then and there through the app.

"I'd like to order 4,000 lattes to go please!" said Steve Jobs on the phone.

He then said; *"No just kidding, wrong number. Thank you. Bye-bye."* (Dubey, 2021).

I really wanted a latte, but I was more amazed at what that little device in Jobs's hand was capable of doing. The rest, as you know, is history.

Some "Did You Know?" Random Tech Facts

Heard of Hedy Lamarr the actress?

Maybe not. She was an actress during your great-grandparents' youth, but it's important to know about her because while the Austrian-born American actress was very talented and acted in over 30 movies, she was also an inventor! She invented a basic version of frequency-hopping communication technology. What's that, you wonder? Well, it was a kind of initial version, or the blueprint, for what we now call Wi-Fi, GPS, and Bluetooth. That was one smart lady!

The logo on Firefox

Firefox is the nickname given to the red panda, an endangered species that looks more like a fox than a panda.

There seems to have been a breakdown in communication when the name Firefox was used for the web browser Mozilla Firefox as everyone thought 'firefox' meant a red fox.

And so, to uncomplicate things, the name Firefox was matched with the picture of a fox instead of a red panda because it made it easier for people to connect the name with the logo, although technically firefox is still the nickname that refers to the red panda—cool fact!

Screen crazy!

Now here's a wacky fact: people in the US have more screens (including TVs, laptops, smartphones, etc.) in their homes than the number of people who live there.

Nokia was a toilet paper seller

Before Nokia went on to become a premier phone brand, the company sold toilet paper, vehicle tires, computers, and different types of electronics; this was in the 1960s.

By the 1980s, the company had failed in just about all fields except for its branch of telecommunication, and so Nokia joined Motorola to help launch the mobile phone industry in the 1980s and went on to become one of the biggest brands in mobile phones. However, Nokia's fame as a top mobile phone brand was short-lived, and although they still have Nokia phones on the market, they are hardly as popular as the famous brands you and I are familiar with.

The number of mobile phones is greater than the number of toilets across the world

There are some places where you will be able to find a mobile phone more easily than a toilet—no matter how urgently you need to use the facilities.

A 2014 survey conducted by UNICEF found that mobile phones are owned by over 6 billion people of the world's population, while only 4.5 billion have access to a toilet (*BRINK Editorial Staff*, 2014).

On the flip-side, mobile phones carry more bacteria than a toilet seat

Now I am not the type of canine to drink out of the toilet, but let me tell you that according to this study, a mobile phone has more bacteria on it than the seat of your toilet. Eeeewwww.

A recent study found that cell phones belonging to high school students had over 17,000 varieties of bacteria crawling on them—gross! (*Kõljalg et al.*, 2017).

This happens because we are always carrying our phones in our hands, and our hands contain a variety of microbes that are not really harmful or disease-causing. But once mixed with the oil secreted from your skin, the microbes multiply on your phone and turn into various types of bacteria. The good news is they are not always harmful. Phew, thank goodness for that. But it is a good idea to wash your hands after using a cell phone belonging to someone else and to avoid carrying one around in your hand all the time.

Modern Technology and Its Evolution - Good to Know Facts

Technology helps to improve our lives, and throughout history, we have had some great inventors come up with amazing inventions that are now a part of our daily lives. Let's look at a few modern technological inventions that have helped shape the world today.

The Assembly Line

The assembly line is an important tool that manufacturers use to meet the high demands of consumers. Producing goods in very large quantities in double quick time is how an assembly line works. For example, have you seen how cars are put together one part at a time on a long assembly line? Each worker has one task to perform and puts together one part of the car as parts move along a conveyor belt.

Henry Ford perfected the assembly line

The concept of mass-producing cars was thought up by none other than the great Henry Ford. Credited with fine-tuning the assembly line, Ford introduced the very first moving assembly line on December 1, 1913. An entire car used to take 12 hours to produce, but on the super quick assembly line, a single could be produced in just one hour and 33 minutes—awesome!

The motivation behind mass-producing cars was Henry Ford's desire to offer cars that were affordable because he wanted just about everyone to own one. And so he decided to break down the manufacture of his Model T car into 84 steps and got each worker to put together one part of it. And that's how the automobile assembly line was made perfect in the US.

Robots soon took over and replaced people who worked the assembly

lines. Many jobs were lost, but manufacturers found the robots convenient as they worked independently and quickly, and were able to operate and manage the single tasks efficiently without making a mistake.

Energy and How it Evolved

Solar energy

Solar energy was harnessed by scientists at the start of the 1900s, and different methods were used to make the most of the sun's energy. For example, solar cells were created to harness and store the sun's energy much like recharging a battery. Stored solar energy is used for many tasks such as generating electricity and heating water.

 Solar panels installed on the roofs of your home and other buildings contain cells that harness and store the sun's energy; that energy is then used to generate electricity throughout the structure.

Nuclear energy

Atoms make up just about everything around us and are the smallest unit of matter. Plasma, solids, gas, and liquids are all made up of tiny atoms which cluster together and are held in place by very strong energy.

Scientists have found a way to harness the energy which holds atoms together. It is called "nuclear energy" and was first used to create the atom bomb in the US, which was responsible for ending World War II (WWII).

J. Robert Oppenheimer created the atom bomb (A-bomb) as one of the world's very first nuclear weapons.

Today, scientists have learned to use nuclear energy for better things such as generating electric power. The atoms are taken apart and that energy is harnessed to generate electricity.

The atoms are split to get at the energy holding them together; scientists call this process "nuclear fission." To generate electricity for our homes, the atoms are split in such a way that the energy is released slowly. But when the atoms are split for a sudden and fast release of their core energy, the result is a huge explosion—that is how the atom bomb works.

Nuclear power plants

Nuclear power plants are used to create nuclear fission and generate energy which, in turn, is used to create heat. The heat then creates steam, which is what runs the giant turbines that generate electricity.

Technology and its Links to Medicine

With the great advances scientists made in the 1900s, technology was soon used to help the medical field as new devices that helped people deal with certain disabilities were invented.

Machines to help our bodies work better

Hearing aids help people with hearing impairments to hear; pacemakers are electrical devices inserted inside a person's body to help their heart to beat at a regular pace, while a dialysis machine, when fixed outside the body, helps people with kidneys that do not function properly to purify their blood.

All these and more amazing machines were built to help people beat diseases and live longer because of developments in technology.

Gene therapy

We can better explain it as genetic engineering.

A gene is a tiny unit located inside the cells of all living things that contain information about how those cells work. They also have a code containing information about the organism it came from (called DNA). Scientists have learned to split genes and attach them to other genes thus creating a new code of information that may help to cure different diseases and even create plants that will thrive and grow without the disease.

Okay, kids, let's see what else you can find out on your own about modern technology. Now it's time for my evening run in the park because I simply love the outdoors. While outside, let's move on to chapter 2, one of my favorite subjects, *Wildlife and Nature.*

Chapter 2: Wildlife & Nature

Planet Earth is blessed with the most amazing collection of wildlife.

Beautiful soaring birds, majestic beasts that are both fearsome and gentle, exotic marine animals living deep within the oceans, fascinating creepy crawlies and insects in all shapes, sizes, and hues.

Simply stepping out into your backyard or local park is enough to discover insects and maybe a rabbit, a mole, and even furry squirrels scurrying about.

The world of animals becomes even more fascinating when you learn special facts about the different species that live on our beautiful planet.

For example, did you know that although I am a dog, I love bananas more than meat? Oh, yes, I love them so much I would trade my best steak for a banana pie.

But on a more serious note, friends, my adventures across the world have taught me so much about animals, the environment they live in, how fierce or adorable they can be, and of course, the types of foods they eat, from herbivores to carnivores to omnivores like me who are not too picky; animals enjoy varied diets.

Are you ready to set off on the adventure of a lifetime exploring the animal kingdom with me?

Fascinating Facts About Dogs

Of course, I must start off by telling you more about everybody's favorite furry best friend, the dog. Here are some truly paw-some facts about your four-legged friends you will find fantastically fascinating.

Dogs are an evolved species of wolf

Dogs were domesticated (or made into pets) by men almost 20,000 years ago. But dogs were not the cute furry pets you know today; the first species of dogs to be tamed by men were very close to wolves. However, in time we evolved and changed, our paws got smaller, and the shape of our skulls changed. Oh yes, and our teeth even started to look more friendly and less like the big bad wolf in Little Red Riding Hood.

This change took place because we were no longer a wild species having to hunt for food. Instead, we had warm cozy fires to lie in front of, a kind master to offer us food, and we had discovered belly rubs. In exchange, we became loyal companions and traded in our ferocious wolf looks for the cuter, but still, fierce guard-dog type features we possess today (except maybe those fluffy French poodles whom I highly suspect are not descendants of wolves).

Dogs are super smart!

Of course, we are, but did you know that a dog is capable of learning over 165 gestures and even words? (Jung et al., 2022).

That's right, a dog has the intelligence of a two-and-a-half-year-old child and is even easier to train!

This intelligence will differ according to species. I wish I could say that French bulldogs are the smartest species, but we are not. I am the exception of course. But the smartest dog breeds are ranked as follows (Cahn, 2022).

1. Border collie
2. Poodle (aha, so there is intelligence under all those curls!)
3. German shepherd
4. Golden retriever
5. Doberman pinscher
6. Shetland sheepdog
7. Labrador retriever
8. Papillon
9. Rottweiler
10. Australian cattle dog

A dog can detect scents forty times better than humans

That's quite true, dogs have an excellent sense of smell. Dogs can even pick up the scent of someone a few days after it was left. This is why dogs make excellent detectives and are often used to help police detect criminals by investigating a crime scene, and even sniff out smugglers at the airport.

✦ For example, a dachshund (that breed of dog that looks like a Weiner) has around 125 million scent receptors while your human nose only has 5 million scent receptors (*Jung et al.*, 2022).

The bloodhound has the best sense of smell among all dog breeds. This ability is so renowned that a bloodhound's detection of an incriminating scent can even be used as evidence in a court of law.

Isn't that just amazing?

A person can even be put in jail simply by being smelled out by a smart bloodhound for carrying banned substances like narcotics or explosives.

Dogs even have much superior hearing to humans and can hear high-pitched sounds humans cannot hear. Plus, we can hear noises from very far away.

Sadly, a dog has a poor sense of taste

Ever wonder why your dog eats smelly old slippers as enthusiastically as he would his kibble?

Well, a dog has very poor taste receptors. If we were to compare you and me, a dog has around 1,700 taste buds while a human has about 9,000. It doesn't matter really; it simply means we can enjoy any meal without making much of a fuss.

FUN FACT!

Some dogs are excellent swimmers. The Newfoundland breed is the best in water and often work as lifeguards and rescue dogs around bodies of water.

A Newfoundland named Whizz, who worked for the Royal Navy, was even awarded the PDSA Order of Merit because he saved a total of nine people while working as a rescue dog at sea.

A dog sweats from its paws

Dogs do not sweat from their tongues, contrary to popular belief. Instead, they sweat from their paws. Our sweat is also a bit more oily than humans' and can be smelled mostly only by other dogs. But get this: many people I know confess to getting a cheesy popcorn kind of smell from their dog's paws—what?!

Unlike humans, dogs do not regulate their body heat by sweating. Instead, they must pant to cool down. That is why your dog sits with its tongue hanging, out breathing heavily right after a vigorous run. By panting, dogs are able to evaporate moisture through their tongues, the passages inside their nose, and their lungs; as air passes over these tissues, their bodies cool down.

The Ancient Egyptians treated dogs like companions

When I met the great Cleopatra in Egypt, she made sure I had my own room and a golden bed to lie in and bask under the sun all day. I even helped her engineers figure out the calculations for some of the temples they were building.

I met the very beautiful Anaksun the Saluki in Cleopatra's palace. The saluki dog breed was the most respected of dog breeds, and Anaksun even had her own servants to look after her every need. She even had a golden necklace and invited me to eat some of her food which were the finest cuts of meat found in Egypt! She told me that when she died, she would be buried in a pyramid beside her master.

Some dogs are super fast!

Dogs are faster than humans because they are made to run around and chase a quarry, just like the wolves who went hunting with their human masters 20,000 years ago. The greyhound is the fastest dog breed and is credited with being able to reach an amazing 45 mph within a few seconds.

Get this kids, the greyhound could easily outdo a cheetah in a race. While a cheetah boasts 70 mph, it can maintain that speed for only 30 seconds, but a greyhound can keep running for seven miles non-stop at a speed of about 35 mph and will easily overtake the exhausted cheetah along the way.

More Dog Facts!

1. Each dog's nose print is unique, just like your fingerprint. So if you want to identify a specific dog out of the same breed, check its nose print.

2. In the US, over 45% of dogs will end up sleeping in their owner's bed.

3. Dogs dream, that's why you see us running or barking in our sleep. Senior dogs and puppies dream the most.

4. The largest dog species, the English mastiff, can weigh between 150–230 pounds.

Awesome Facts About Great White Sharks

 Okay, kids, time for some thrills and shakes as we learn about the ocean's greatest predator—the Great White Shark.

Fearsome, and totally fascinating, these deadly hunters certainly deserve our respect.

Great whites live in all oceans

These predators can be found across the globe in just about every ocean, although they prefer cooler waters and hang out close to the coast.

 Classified as the largest predatory fish species, great whites will grow to around 4.6 meters on average, although people have come across great whites that are 6 meters long.

The great white is fast

This mighty hunter can travel at astounding speeds of 60 kilometers per hour! So the chances of outswimming one are pretty slim. Their very powerful tail fin and streamlined body shape help them to maintain their speed. The shark's white-colored underbelly is what earns it part of its name. I don't have to explain the 'great' part, now do I?

The great whites have scary teeth

No dentist is ever getting close to the great white because it has close to five rows of teeth, amounting to about 300 very pointy, very sharp teeth. But get this, humans are not its favorite meal. Yes, there is the reported attack now and then, but scientists say this is more out of curiosity, with the shark wondering what this funny-looking thing splashing about in the water tastes like. However, it is no fun getting eaten by one, and my advice is to practice caution at all times.

Great whites are very cunning

Victims often never even know they are being chased by a great white until it pops out of the water and dives down with a mouthful of whatever it was stalking. The great white is a stealthy hunter and will circle its prey from below. It will then shoot out of the water, in what scientists call a "breech position," before grabbing the startled prey and heading to the depths of the ocean. Ooh, that sent shivers down my spine and my fur is standing on end!

Great whites are the worst parents

That's right—there is no motherly love given to babies from a mama great white. The sharks usually give birth to anywhere between 2-10 babies, called pups. As soon as they are born, the great

white pups will swim away and try to take care of themselves because hanging around mom could result in them getting eaten. Yikes!

The great white's greatest enemy is man

The great white is at the top of the food chain and is not challenged by many other marine life except for the orca (killer whale). Therefore, it has the potential to enjoy a long and healthy survival as a species.

However, that may not end up to be the case. Sadly, humans are responsible for the number of these fascinating creatures getting reduced. Overfishing and even illegal hunting of the great white have led to its numbers dwindling. And I regret to inform you, kids, that the great white has now made it to the International Union of Conservation of Nature (IUCN) Red List of Vulnerable Species.

Did you know that there are tireless marine biologists working hard to protect and conserve the great whites? These special people are responsible for protecting and learning about much of the planet's oceans and marine life. Would you like to be a marine biologist when you grow up?

Top Turtle Facts that Are Turtle-ly Awesome

Turtles are amongst the most fascinating of all marine creatures and are found in many shapes, colors, and sizes. They are  found around the world, surviving in different environments, and belong to the Testudines reptile group including giant tortoises, snappy little freshwater terrapins, and magnificent sea turtles.

Turtles are amongst the oldest from the reptile family

That's right, turtles are even older than alligators, crocodiles, and snakes, which all belong to the reptile family. Turtles actually existed when dinosaurs roamed the Earth almost 200 million years ago! That makes the species really old and one of our planet's most cherished life forms.

All turtles have a hard shell

Tortoises, terrapins, and turtles all have a hard cartilaginous shell as their trademark. This bony structure located outside their body is super tough and offers protection from predators. While not all turtles can, there are some in the species like the tortoise, that are able to tuck their entire head back into their shells thus avoiding getting hurt by predatory animals.

A turtle's skeleton is on the outside

How awesome is that, right?

A turtle's shell is really its skeleton and is located on the outside of its body. The shell is not just one big bone, although it may look like that. It is, in fact, made up of over 50 bones, and they include the animal's rib cage as well as its vertebra—all located on the outside.

A turtle's shell grows with it, ensuring the turtle never grows too big for its shell. Plus, unlike the turtles you see in most cartoons, actual turtles cannot step out of its shell, as it is fused to the turtle's body.

fun fact

The largest species of turtle is the leatherback sea turtle. It is also called the lute, or leathery turtle. A fully grown leatherback will be about two meters long and weigh a staggering 600 kg.

Turtles eat a lot of different things

A turtle's diet really depends on where it lives. Freshwater species like terrapins will eat things like fruits, grass, or even juicy bugs. Sea turtles will eat jellyfish, squid, and even sea algae. Because of their varied diets, turtles belong to all three food groups. Some turtles are herbivores which means they eat only plants, others are carnivores and prefer to eat only meat, but most turtles are omnivores and will eat a mix of both plant food and meat.

Turtles belong to the amniotes group

Birds, reptiles, and some mammals are classified as amniotes. This means they reproduce in the form of eggs, which are laid on land although the animals may live in both water and on land. Turtles, too, can live in water, but they lay their eggs on land.

Turtles are cold-blooded

Turtles are also cold-blooded reptiles and enjoy a very long life span. Jonathan, who lives on the island of St. Helena, is the oldest turtle on record.

He was brought to St Helena from Seychelles in 1882, as a gift for Sir William Gray Wilson. While it is believed that Jonathan was born in 1832, and turns 190 years in 2022, there is speculation he could be older. Maybe I will visit Jonathan and have a chat with him to see how old he really is.

Before Jonathan, the oldest turtle to be recorded lived on the island of Tonga. It was named Tu' i Malila and lived for 188 years.

Turtles are endangered

Just like the great white shark, most turtle and tortoise species are on the endangered species list. According to the IUCN, 129 species from amongst the 300-odd types of tortoise and turtle species on our planet are either endangered, vulnerable, or on the critical list of becoming extinct.

The main reasons for this shocking state of affairs are attributed to turtles losing their natural habitats due to the development of land, poaching, and of course, the very bad and illegal trade of pets.

Remember kids, extinct is forever, and you must never encourage any of the actions which lead to the loss of yet another animal species. You can help by starting small and discouraging your friends from keeping endangered turtle species as pets. They belong in the wild where scientists can protect and help them thrive.

Project Idea!

Gather facts about turtles and make a poster to hang up in school so your friends can learn more about this ancient but endangered species before it's too late.

The next time you go to a tropical location on holiday, like Sri Lanka or the Maldives, make sure to ask your parents to take you snorkeling where you will be able to spot sea turtles.

Fun and Hoppy Frog Facts

Frogs have fascinated me ever since I woke up with one sitting on the tip of my nose. Frogs are a good indication of how good the surrounding environment is: The better and less polluted a place is, the more frogs you will find. With over 4,000 species, frogs certainly give us a lot to talk about.

I know several children who keep frogs as pets, while the pond in my human friend's backyard is home to a lovely family of frogs who enjoy croaking all night, especially after a big rain.

Frogs are everywhere

There are more than 4,000 varieties of frogs on our planet. The exact numbers are unclear as scientists keep discovering new species. They can be found in a variety of colors, shapes, and sizes.

The largest frog species is the Goliath frog

In the wild, a Goliath frog will weigh around 7 pounds and can grow to lengths of about 12 inches. If you visit the Fish and Amphibian section of the zoo, you can see these large frogs. But sadly the Goliath frog has been on the endangered list of the IUCN since 2004. The reasons are many: deforestation, losing their habitats when dams are constructed, and even being hunted by humans who enjoy eating the Goliath frog.

Frogs can be toxic

Did you know that some tropical frogs are colored in a certain way to let predators know that they are poisonous? Yikes! They will be colored in shades of blue, yellow, orange, green, and red as a message to predators who think they look yummy—the message says "I'm very poisonous, so stay away!" The colors protect the frogs and are indeed an indication they are poisonous. I found out the golden poison dart frog is poisonous enough to kill around 20,000 mice!

Frogs can jump really high

Have you ever chased a frog? Then you know how high it can jump. In fact, on average a frog is able to jump more than 20 times its height, but some can jump even higher.

Check out the frog's ears to know if it is male or female

Now here's a rather quirky fact about frogs. You can tell if they are a boy or girl frog by looking at their ears. Called the 'tympanum,' a frog's ears are situated right behind its eyes. Check it out, and if you notice the ear is larger than the eye, then it is a male frog. If the tympanum is smaller than the eye, it's a girl frog.

Frogs eat their own skin

I find this totally gross, but it is a natural phenomenon for frogs. You see, frogs shed their skin once a week or even every day. It's called 'molting,' and when a frog molts or sheds its skin, it goes ahead and eats it because it is full of proteins, and they don't want to waste any of the goodness found there. A frog will actually start rubbing off its old skin straight into its mouth, unlike snakes which wriggle out of their old skin and leave it behind. You can actually find some cool videos of frogs shedding their skin (molting) right into their mouths and then eating it if you search online.

Frogs drink and breathe through their skin

That's right, I once invited a frog over for some lemonade, and he immediately hopped right into the glass of water I offered! Because you see, frogs do not drink water from those great big mouths. Instead, they absorb water through their skin.

Frogs have what scientists call a "permeable skin," which means it is capable of allowing gasses and liquids to pass through it, much like a strainer. Therefore, frogs also breathe through their skin by absorbing the oxygen in the water.

While this is a good system for always staying cool and hydrated when in water, the permeable skin of a frog can also work against it.

For example, if the pond or lake a frog lives in is polluted, its skin will absorb all the toxic poisons there and kill the frog. Also, when a frog is out of water for too long, moisture will leak out of its permeable skin and the poor frog will become dehydrated.

We must make sure to never pollute waterways by throwing any type of junk in them. There are many species of animals living in water, and they are very vulnerable to poisons put there by uncaring human beings.

Frogs can even drown

Frogs can drown because, like you and me, they have lungs through which they breathe. They are careful though, making sure they do not get water in their lungs because that would cause them to drown. Like I said before, they can even breathe through their skin, but they can only absorb the amount of oxygen present in the water they are in, and sometimes that oxygen is not enough, which means frogs must come up for air.

What causes a frog to have slimy skin?

A frog's permeable skin has a lot to do with it actually. Some frogs have a thick mucus coating protecting their skin. This mucus, which is very slimy, will help the frog to retain the moisture in its skin. It also contains antibacterial properties which guard against the absorption of some toxins that can harm the frog.

There are even types of frogs that produce a kind of waxy substance which they then spread on their body to help lock in the moisture and keep them cool. If a frog plans to spend the day exploring, he will spread this waxy substance to help him remain cool.

Frogs lay eggs in the darndest of places

Not all frogs go ahead and lay eggs in water. Oh, no, it's much more complicated than that. Since frog eggs do not have a hard shell like normal eggs, they can easily dry up or get squished. So, to protect their eggs, frogs have come up with some genius methods.

Frogs lay their eggs under leaves that are located above a body of water, especially in rainforests. Once the eggs hatch, the little tadpoles fall right into the water and begin their journey of survival as they start to evolve into baby froglets.

The male species of the Darwin frog swallows the eggs, but not to eat it as food. It plants the eggs in its vocal sac, located in the frog's throat, and those eggs remain safe and snug until they are ready to hatch. This amazing phenomenon works after the female Darwin frog has laid about 40 eggs amongst leaves close to water. The male frog then takes over to watch over the eggs for the next 3–4 weeks. Once he sees the little embryos starting to move, he will ingest them and plant them in his vocal sac until they hatch. Isn't that just the most caring gesture a dad can offer? Look for the amazing videos online.

The female Surinam toad—which is actually a frog but called a toad because of its rough skin—performs an equally amazing feat by hatching her babies right out of the skin on her back. The female Surinam frog has lots of holes on her back, and her eggs get planted there, deep into the skin. Once implanted, the

embryos will develop, turn into tadpoles, and then grow into miniature versions of their mom, which is when they break out of the mom's skin and swim away. There are online videos of this one too kids, but let me warn you—it is freaky and makes me feel itchy all over!

Frogs can see what's behind them

There is no way you can sneak up from behind a frog because they can see from the back of their heads. Did you ever wonder about the size of a frog's eyes? Why are they so big?

Well, a frog's eyes are located at the top of their head and stick out so far to allow them to rotate them almost 360 degrees; this allows them to see to the sides and back of their head without even turning around—awesome! I wish I had eyes that rotated 360 degrees.

Frogs' eyes have an even more awesome feature which is the nictitating membrane—a third eyelid. This eyelid, or membrane, closes over the eye

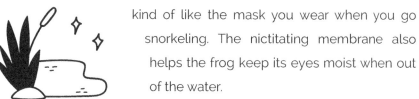

to protect it but allows the frog to see underwater—kind of like the mask you wear when you go snorkeling. The nictitating membrane also helps the frog keep its eyes moist when out of the water.

Animals That Spread Disease and Are Dangerous to People

There are many animals that pose a threat to humans. Some are poisonous like snakes and scorpions, while others carry disease and germs.

The mosquito

Mosquitoes are dangerous to humans. They can be carriers of many bacteria, viruses, and parasites. Some diseases spread to humans from mosquitoes can be fatal and even results in a pandemic. A pandemic happens when the disease spreads across the world and is hard to contain.

Mosquitoes spread diseases such as malaria, filaria, yellow fever, Zika virus, and dengue. They thrive more in tropical conditions, and it is important to take along insect repellent whenever you are visiting an area that has mosquitoes.

Dengue is one of the widest spread diseases caused by mosquitoes. Tropical countries are having a tough time dealing with dengue which can be curtailed by keeping one's environment clean and free of places that collect water.

Most poisonous creatures

Which do you think is worse: a spider or a snake? While both are important to maintain the balance of our planet's ecosystem, it is important to treat these animals with respect.

The most venomous spider in the world is called the funnel-web spider

There are two species, the tree-dwelling funnel-web, and the Sydney funnel-web. Both are highly poisonous and can be fatal. This spider is native to Australia.

The most venomous jellyfish is the box jellyfish

There are 51 types of box jellyfish, but only four varieties are poisonous. I once encountered one while bathing in the sea close to the Great Barrier Reef in Australia. Luckily, I recognized it from its box shape and managed to steer clear of it—whew! Many people fall victim to the sting of this jellyfish, especially in a country called the Philippines.

The most venomous snake is the saw-scaled viper

On the North American continent, the most venomous snake is the rattlesnake. Even more venomous is the saw-scaled viper, also called the carpet viper.

This snake is found in hot climates such as the Middle East, Africa,

Pakistan, Sri Lanka, and India.

But you know what kids? Just because the tropics are home to some of nature's more dangerous creatures, it should not be avoided. The tropics are home to some of the most beautiful locations in the world.

I once visited the beautiful island of Sri Lanka, located on the Indian Ocean, and it had the most beautiful golden sandy beaches where I built sandcastles and basked in the sun all day. There are many sunny and warm locations in our world that you should make an effort to learn about. Who knows, you may become a traveler like me who decides to explore the world.

The most venomous insect in the world is the harvester ant

The Maricopa harvester ant is the only venomous kind of its species. This ant's sting is 35 times more poisonous than a rattlesnake's. The pain from the bite of this ant is quite intense and can last up to eight hours. The venomous harvester ant is found in Arizona, Mexico, Texas, Nevada, and other hot states.

Quick Weird and Wacky Animal Facts

Did you know that kangaroos, who come from Australia, cannot walk backward?

Well, they simply cannot. It's because they move by hopping around. That movement is called 'saltation'. The large kangaroo will hop with both its very big feet at the same time, using its large tail to maintain its balance. I guess hopping backward is an impossibility.

Emus, who are also from Australia, are large flightless birds similar to the ostrich. However, unlike the ostrich, the emu cannot walk backward. The reason for this is still not clear to researchers.

Don't you go asking your pet pig to enjoy the sunset unless it decides to lie on its back and look up into the sky!

You see, a pig's physical structure and placement of its neck muscles make it impossible for the creature to turn its head up to look at the sky.

A flamingo can only eat with its head upside down

 It's true, boys and girls; a flamingo has bristles on the top of its top beak and those bristles help it to filter out all the mud that gets into its mouth while eating food. But to use those bristles on the top of its beak, the flamingo must turn its head upside down.

Panda droppings (poop) are made into paper

Pandas live on a diet of eco-friendly bamboo plants, and so the National Panda Reserve in Sichuan has struck a deal to start using the panda poo to make recycled paper.

Dolphins are really weird

For starters, when a dolphin sleeps, it will only shut
down one half of its brain; the other half remains
alert to make sure the dolphin does not drown in
its sleep. As a mammal, the dolphin must come
up for air, and despite being able to hold its breath
underwater for a long time, it must still come up to
breathe. And so part of its brain remains alert even in sleep
mode to ensure the dolphin wakes up in time to come up for a breath
of air.

A cockroach can go on living even without its head because its brain is actually located in its body!

Amazing right? So, even if it loses its head, the poor roach will go about
as usual, eventually dying of starvation because without its head, it has
no mouth to eat!

A shrimp's heart, on the other hand, is located inside its head

This is because a shrimp's body is divided into two,
the head and tail.

A snail can sleep for over three years

A snail will go into hibernation if the environment is not right and does
not offer enough moisture for it to survive. They dislike winter, for

example, and could end up sleeping for almost three years.

A slug does not have a nose, instead, it has four tentacles.

Two of which function like a nose helping it to smell smells that are far away, and the other two located on top of its head are the slug's eyes which help it to see.

Did you know that the kiwi bird is almost blind?

That's right, not only is this poor bird incapable of flying, but it can't see too well either. Here are some fun facts about the kiwi:

The kiwi is the bird with nostrils located at the end of its beak.

It has feathers, but they are more like fur, and even molt every year. No wonder they can't fly.

It has no tail feathers but does have whiskers similar to your kitty cat.

The kiwi is nocturnal, which means it is an animal that is active at nighttime. And while most nocturnal animals have excellent eyesight, the kiwi doesn't see too well with its tiny little eyes.

Instead, the kiwi has amazing senses of smell and hearing that are beyond exceptional. No sneaking up on this bird! (Or could it be a cat? I really can't say.)

Someone actually recorded the flight of a chicken, and the longest nonstop flight of a chicken was 13 seconds

That is how long that bird could flap and fly. The study was conducted in 2014, and I believe no one has been interested in testing a chicken's flight since then.

However, in defense of the poor chicken, I also found out that domestically-bred chickens are engineered to grow larger breasts—you know, for meat purposes (now try not to get upset)—and this extra weight on their breasts prevents them from a proper flight.

The domestic chicken descends from the red jungle fowl, a magnificent and rather fierce bird. The jungle fowl lives in the wild and hunts for food on the ground but roosts (which means where a bird settles to rest) in treetops which keeps it safe from predators. You guessed it, the red jungle fowl can run and fly pretty well—unlike its poor cousin the domestic chicken.

An elephant cannot jump

And a good thing too, as the largest land mammal, I don't think we would enjoy the vibrations caused by an elephant jumping. An adult elephant will weigh somewhere around 16,000 pounds and is simply too heavy to jump. Even when they are running at full speed, they never have all four legs off the ground. You see kids, when running there is a point when all four or two legs of an animal or human being are off the ground for a split second, in a kind of jumping motion. Just watch Usain Bolt, the world's fastest man running, in really slow motion and you will see what I mean.

So, my conclusion is that an elephant is actually an expert power-walker and never really runs. Power walkers do not lift all feet off the ground at the same time because that would mean they are running. And really with its huge size, the elephant really has no reason to want to run away in fear. He could simply stomp down on his predators. Although the elephants I have met are really very gentle creatures.

FUN NATURE FACTS TO ASTOUND YOU

I love the outdoors—running in open fields, splashing in the lakes, building sandcastles on the beach, and accompanying my human friend on scenic mountain treks. Our planet certainly is stunning and provides all the amazing wildlife and humans with the perfect home.

On my adventures, I gathered a lot of fun facts about nature that I want to share with you so that you understand how special our planet Earth is. Animals, plants, and the landscape all make up nature and are not a part of man-made structures. Nature in its pure form is beautiful, fierce, and totally fascinating.

Quirky and Fascinating Nature Trivia

Microscopic marine plants in the Arctic

In 2011, NASA was quite surprised to find evidence of microscopic marine plants, called phytoplankton, thriving below the three-foot-thick chunk of ice of the Arctic! This icy area is in fact home to the richest growth of microscopic marine plant life than any of the oceans across the world. Don't you agree our planet is awesome? NASA says the one reason this phenomenon takes place is the greenhouse effect, which is thinning the ice in the Arctic and allowing sunlight to reach and nurture the plants growing there.

The largest flower on our planet

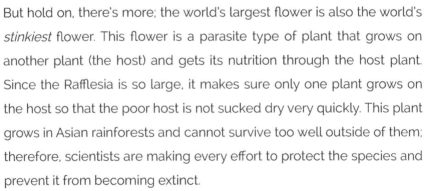

The largest flower on our planet is the Rafflesia arnoldii. This flower weighs a whopping 20 pounds and will grow to about three feet in diameter. Imagine the size of the vase you would need to put this flower in!

But hold on, there's more; the world's largest flower is also the world's *stinkiest* flower. This flower is a parasite type of plant that grows on another plant (the host) and gets its nutrition through the host plant. Since the Rafflesia is so large, it makes sure only one plant grows on the host so that the poor host is not sucked dry very quickly. This plant grows in Asian rainforests and cannot survive too well outside of them; therefore, scientists are making every effort to protect the species and prevent it from becoming extinct.

Fruit with seeds on the outside!

The only fruit with seeds on the outside is the strawberry. On average, one berry will have around 200 seeds. Would you have the patience to count them? Each seed is considered a whole fruit by botanists who also say strawberries belong to the rose family. To check out this theory, I actually went in search of a strawberry plant and smelled it; they got it right all right, strawberries smell as sweet as roses.

The most widely grown fruit is the strawberry, and in the US, the average person eats about eight pounds of strawberries each year. Most kids will choose the strawberry as their favorite fruit.

In fact, the US produces the world's largest number of strawberries; Oregon, Florida, and California are the top producers. And while strawberries are rich in nutrients such as vitamin C, fiber, antioxidants, and potassium, they can also cause severe illnesses if not cultivated with care.

Strawberries have been linked to the spread of many illnesses in the US including Hepatitis A, Norovirus, and E-coli. So kids, you must take precautions before eating strawberries. Make sure to wash them well, and only buy strawberries from reliable sellers.

Okay kids, I hope you enjoyed this chapter learning about how awesome our planet and its inhabitants are. Next, let's look at a few interesting facts about human biology.

Chapter 3: Human Biology

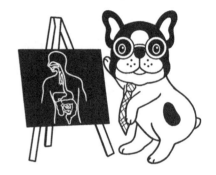

Hey kiddos, now it's time to learn about your body, how it works, and how it grows. You will be amazed at the wondrous facts I discovered about the human body. And I must say that, from a dog's point of view, it certainly is awesome.

QUICK AND AWESOME HUMAN BIOLOGY FACTS

The human body emits a little bit of light!

It's way too small an amount to see, but it's there! It would be correct

 to say that the human body glows. The levels of light produced by your body will rise or fall depending on the time of day. The light is 1,000 times less sensitive than the range your eyes can detect, which is why people cannot see the light surrounding each other. Scientists are not really sure about the cause of this light but believe it is a biochemical reaction caused by free radicals.

Biochemical reactions happen when there are reactions inside the cells of your body. Free radicals, boys and girls, are unstable molecules found in your body. They are constantly looking for other molecules to bond with and sometimes cause disease and damage to cells.

Did you know the human brain is mostly water?

That's right, almost 75% of your brain is made up of water (*The Human Brain*, 2022).

An average person's belly button will carry about 67 types of bacteria

Scientists conducted tests and found that while some people's belly buttons had about 29 types of bacteria, others had around 107. As the least-cleaned part of the human body, the belly button is a hot spot and hub for bacteria to grow. So, remember to wash those belly buttons next time you have a bath, kids.

The word 'muscle' in Latin translates to "little mouse"

Do you know why? It's because small muscles actually reminded people of a small mouse!

Through shedding, a person loses around 8.8 pounds of dead skin cells every year

And you know what? There are trillions of dust mites in your home, all eating the dead skin flakes dropped by you and your family. There are several layers to your skin, and the one on top is called the 'epidermis.' The epidermis is made up of a substance called 'keratin,' which is

also what your nails and hair are made of. In other animals, keratin forms hooves, shells on turtles, claws, and horns. The individual keratin cells are called 'keratinocytes,' and as they grow the ones on top will die and fall off.

Your nerves carry information to your brain, but how do they inform your brain the moment you step on a pin?

Well, just like fiber optics taking information across phone lines at super-fast speeds, your nerves can send information across your body at speeds of 100 miles an hour. How awesome is that?

On average, the human heart will beat over 3 billion times during an entire lifespan

In one day the heart will beat about 100,000 times. Isn't the heart an amazing organ?

A person will fart an average of fourteen times a day. (Maybe dogs do a little more than that.)

Did you also know that your fart is pretty fast and will travel at around 10 feet per second? How fast can you fart and leave a room before you're found out?

Your teeth may not be as sharp as a great white shark's, but they are just as strong

In fact, your wisdom teeth, the ones located at the back, are as strong as sharks' teeth. Scientists have found out that the enamel coating on human teeth is very similar to the enamel coating on sharks' teeth, making them just as strong.

Did you know that dogs are not the only good smellers of smells?

The human nose is able to sniff out and tell the difference between a trillion types of smells. How many smells can you name? My favorite is the smell of banana bread being baked!

About 7-8% of your body's weight is from your blood

 An average person has about 5 liters of blood in their body. Because of this, your body can manage to lose a small percentage of blood and survive until a blood transfusion can be done. However, losing over 15% of your total blood volume could cause a person to go into a shock.

Your mouth will produce over a liter, or maybe two, of spit (aka, saliva) within one day

Now, who do you think drools the most, me or you? Well, in truth dogs do, but if you were to collect all the spit that forms in your mouth within a day, you would have a liter, maybe more.

Find out how tall you are!

Stretch your arms out and measure the length from the fingertips of one hand, to the end of the fingertips on the other hand. Try it!

I tried measuring myself from the tip of my nose to the tip of my tail, but that was not my correct height because the method only works for people. A French bulldog is only about 11–13 inches tall.

You simply cannot sneeze and have your eyes open at the same time 👁

It's a proven fact. They close for even a split second during that sneeze. Now, if you make a very conscious effort to keep your eyes open while sneezing, it is possible, but it is all an automatic reflex and happens really fast.

Human Biology Trivia

See how many questions you can answer. Give yourself one point for each correct answer. The answers are on the next page. Get yourself a paper and pencil and let's get started!

1. True or false: The largest percentage of dust in your house is made up of dead human skin.
2. Yes or no: The adult human has 206 bones while a baby has 300 bones.
3. Does a person grow taller in space?
4. Name the hardest substance found on the human body.
5. True or false: During the process of digesting food, the temperature of your body will increase.
6. Which human blood type is the rarest?
7. Why does your eyesight start to get weaker as you get older?
8. Which part of your body is called the 'pinna'?
9. Do your ears continue to grow throughout your lifespan?
10. True or false: Neanderthals had larger brains than modern men.

Okay, friends, time to tally up your points. Turn to the next page for the answers. Keep in mind that despite your score, you are still a winner because you are reading the answers and learning more about the human body—well done!

Trivia Answers

1. True or false: The largest percentage of dust in your house is made up of dead human skin.

False. Dust in your home is made up of many different particles. Dead human skin is one; others include insect waste, dirt, and even animal dander.

2. Yes or no: The adult human has 206 bones while a baby has 300 bones.

Yes. Some of the bones in a baby's skull are still not fused and will be counted separately. So, an adult human with a completely fused skull will have fewer bones than a baby.

3. Does a person grow taller in space?

Yes. Gravity in space causes a person's cartilage discs in the spine to expand, automatically making them taller.

4. Name the hardest substance found on the human body.

Tooth enamel. Remember human teeth are as strong as a shark's teeth.

5. True or false: During the process of digesting food, the temperature of your body will increase.

True. The process of digestion makes your stomach and other organs work harder than they normally do, causing more energy to be used up which in turn increases your body temperature.

6. Which human blood type is the rarest?

AB negative is the rarest type of blood with only about one percent of the world's population having this blood type. Do you know what your blood type is? Ask your parents!

7. Why does your eyesight start to get weaker as you get older?

The lenses in your eyes continue to grow, and as they grow, they get thicker making it harder for people to see as they age.

8. Which part of your body is called the 'pinna'?

The pinna is your outer ear. The shell-like cartilage part looks like, well, a shell.

9. Do your ears continue to grow throughout your lifespan?

Your bones and muscles stop growing once you reach 18 (or younger for girls). However, your ears and nose are made up of cartilage, which never stops growing. That is why older people seem to have bigger ears and noses. Of course, since people do not have long floppy ears like dogs, you have nothing to worry about because cartilage grows at a very slow pace.

10. True or false: Neanderthals had larger brains than modern men.

True. Scientists have discovered that Neanderthal brains actually kept growing long after they reached maturity, hence they are bigger than modern men. However, scientists are also starting to change previous theories that the Neanderthal man was not very intelligent. Cave art done by this ancient species is starting to prove that Neanderthals may have been more intelligent than we actually give them credit for.

Well, I thoroughly enjoyed that quiz, and I hope you did too and learned more about your body in the process.

In the next chapter, we are going to learn about world geography. I have found interesting facts about volcanoes, the ocean, weather, and more. There is a special story too about a brave little girl called Tilly.

Chapter 4: World Geography

In this chapter about world geography, you will see how diverse our planet is; there are tall mountains like the Himalayas that are exciting and dangerous to explore, wondrous and beautiful formations like the Great Barrier Reef in the ocean, and so much more.

Shall we begin?

 ## MOUNTAIN FACTS

Do you know why planes don't fly over the Himalayas?

There are some areas that planes choose not to fly over such as the Himalayas, the Arctic, and Antarctica. Most often it's not because our modern planes cannot climb to such altitudes; they simply choose not to due to safety reasons.

With regards to the Himalayas, for example, there are several reasons it's dangerous for aircrafts.

Mount Everest is 29,031.69 feet (8,848 meters) high, while the other peaks in the range average at least 20,000 feet. Many commercial aircrafts can climb to heights of 30,000 feet, but to fly over the Himalayas they must soar higher into the stratosphere, which poses many risks including a thinning of oxygen. And if oxygen masks suddenly drop due to potential danger in air quality within the plane, the aircraft must drop to 10,000 feet, and in the Himalayas that is a huge risk (*Curran*, 2020).

Clear air turbulence is another reason. This condition is not always picked up by the plane's radar and is often present in high mountain ranges. Clear air turbulence creates cold weather which can cause the aircraft's fuel to freeze.

The Mount Everest climb is a challenge, and many fail to reach the summit

 Every year, hundreds of people attempt the risky ascent of Mount Everest. However, the Himalayas are not kind to everyone, and many fail in their attempt to get to the summit of Everest.

While many have succeeded, many have failed and even perished on the slopes of the mountain.

People train for months before attempting to climb the mountain, and, still, there are many dangers that make climbs unsuccessful. The thinning oxygen in the atmosphere as people ascend higher means they must carry canisters of oxygen, or they will suffocate and die of exhaustion. Sudden avalanches (which are when a side of the snow covering the mountain comes crashing down) sometimes cover entire teams of climbers.

According to information on the Himalayan database, the chance of someone dying along the way to the summit of Everest is one in every 100. Sometimes people who fall into trouble halfway up the mountain cannot be rescued and are sadly lost to the world forever.

Why can't helicopters fly to Mount Everest?

So kids, you may be wondering why a helicopter can't be sent to rescue people who get into trouble while climbing Mount Everest. After all, helicopters perform many brave rescue operations, right?

Well, the simple fact is that the air density at higher altitudes does not offer the blades in a helicopter enough lift. The highest one can go is Everest camp 2, located at 21,000 feet (6,400.8 meters). So if you ever get into trouble climbing Everest, you must make it back to the camp to get rescued.

What is the longest name given to a place?

Can you pronounce this name?

Taumatawhakatangihangakoauauotamateaturipukakapikimaungahor onukupokaiwhenuakitanatahu

I got my tongue tied up in a knot trying to pronounce it. The name is given to a hill, 1,000 feet high, located on the North Island in New

Zealand. The place, located in Porangahau, holds a place in the Guinness Book of Records as the longest place name at 85 letters.

The indigenous people of New Zealand, the Maori, named this hill in honor of a brave warrior called Tamatea who spent a long time on the hill in sadness after the death of his brother. The hill was named in honor of this act, and the above name is only a shortened version, here is the full name and meaning given to the place.

"The summit where Tamatea, the man with the big knees, the slider, climber of mountains, the land-swallower who traveled about, played his nose flute to his loved one."

Thank goodness my name is just Ronny the Frenchie!

All About Volcanoes

I had to put on my thermal insulation suit for this one because it is really hot inside a volcano! Now let me tell you that no one can get into an active volcano without getting burned, but due to my superpowered brain, I was able to invent my insulated suit and explore more. Here's what I found out, kids:

How do volcanoes form?

An opening in the surface of the Earth is generally how a volcano is formed. You will find volcanoes typically on the top of a mountain range.

Kids, you know that the Earth's core is made up of hot molten lava; well, the opening in the volcano allows this hot lava to get out, as well as other gasses that are trapped beneath the Earth's crust.

Are volcanoes dangerous?

Yes, they are. Volcanoes pose many threats. They can destroy homes, crops, and terrain for many miles. Scientists monitor active volcanoes and send out evacuation notices if there is any sudden activity or threat the volcano will erupt.

When a volcano erupts, there is a flow of very hot toxic substances. Poisonous gas, hot rocks, molten lava, and ash are all a part of a volcanic eruption. It is called a "pyroclastic flow" and travels very fast—450 miles an hour!

Sometimes people cannot get away in time and will perish as a result of pyroclastic flows, although with today's technology scientists are able to issue warnings in time. A volcano eruption is hard to predict, but there are some signs to watch out for: earthquakes and emission of gasses. In the olden days, people were not so lucky and sometimes whole towns perished due to volcanoes suddenly erupting.

Many people live within close proximity to a volcano in what scientists call a "proximity danger zone." Around

350,000 million people are believed to live too close to volcanoes, which, as I calculated, is about one out of every 20 people.

A volcano can occur at different locations due to different reasons. The most common spot for a volcano to occur is the meeting point of the Earth's tectonic plates.

Do you know what tectonic plates are?

Tectonic plates are pieces of the Earth's crust that are broken, meeting at points where the broken points fit together, quite similar to your favorite jigsaw puzzle. Scientists also call tectonic plates "crustal plates," and they can be found in both the ocean and on land. Sometimes these plates are constantly moving and shift into different positions, getting stuck due to friction. Sometimes the plates get unstuck and move, causing a release of energy that moves above the Earth's crust causing earthquakes or tremors.

A volcano often occurs where tectonic plates meet. Since the two plates are simply stuck together and not fused, there is an opening into the Earth's core which causes a volcano when molten lava and gas start to seep out of the crack.

QUICK FACT

Do you know how hot lava can be? 1,250°C, or 2,282°F . That is pretty hot! Enough to cook an egg and burn it in a split second.

Volcanoes are mostly found around the Pacific Ocean within an area scientists call the "Ring of Fire"

Those around the Hawaiian Islands are known as "hot spots." I once visited the islands for a luau (the name given to a traditional Hawaiian celebration), and boy did I enjoy that party!

Pele's curse is why you must never take volcanic rock home

Pele is the Hawaiian Goddess of fire and volcano, and she will curse anyone who takes the volcanic rock from her land. Every year, the Hawaiian post office receives many packages containing lava rock and sand, sent back by people who took them home and experienced very bad luck.

The worst volcanic eruption to date is Mount Tambora, which is in Indonesia

Indonesia is an archipelago (a chain or group of islands in one area). Mount Tabora, located on the island of Sumbawa, erupted in 1815, creating a crater that is over 3,600 feet deep. A plume (smoke that spreads in the shape of a feather) of very hot gas and ash rose almost 28 miles into the sky, affecting surrounding islands, crops, and houses in the area.

Another interesting fact about Indonesia and volcanoes involves the Kawah Ijen volcano on Java Island. At night, people can see an electric blue flow of lava making its way down the slopes of the mountain. But guess what kids? It's not lava at all! The blue glow comes from the sulfuric gasses which combust as they leak through the cracks of the volcano and combine with the atmosphere. The phenomenon is very beautiful with some flames spurting five meters in the air.

INDONESIA

THE OCEAN

The marine biome that is made up of oceans, reefs, corals, and estuaries covers almost three-quarters of the Earth's surface. That's right, our planet has more water bodies than land. But even more amazing is the fact that almost 85% of the planet's plant life is found in the sea!

The Great Barrier Reef

The largest reef system in the world is the Great Barrier Reef in Australia. It is so big that the reef appears in satellite images taken from outer space. The reef is located off the coast of sunny Queensland in Australia and is found within the Coral Sea. The reef is a UNESCO World Heritage Site and is close to 1,250 miles long. The reef in total is 135,000 square miles and is the greatest structure built by living organisms—coral! Isn't that just amazing?

The Dead Sea

The Dead Sea is actually a lake. Located between Jordan and Israel, this lake is a beautiful and mystifying phenomenon. Nothing lives in the Dead Sea apart from some types of algae and microorganisms. The water is ten times saltier than seawater. The Dead Sea is formed by water flowing into it from the River Jordan. However, as it is landlocked, the water cannot flow out anywhere else once it gets into the Dead Sea.

Due to the very hot weather in the region, the water starts to evaporate and leaves behind minerals and salt which then make the remaining water very salty. Scientists say about 37 billion tons of salt are found there. The high salt and mineral content make the dead sea a popular spa, with many people believing in its curative powers, and upon visiting the Dead Sea, you will see lots of people with mud from the lake rubbed all over their bodies. I tried it too, kids, and it made my fur soft and smooth.

Another super feature of this very salty lake is that you can naturally float on the water. Yup, you won't sink! The high salt content makes the lake very buoyant, enabling people to float on the water without sinking.

The tallest mountain in the...sea?

You know that Everest is the tallest mountain in the world, but have you heard of Mauna Kea?

Mount Everest is called the tallest mountain in the world because it stands at a height of 8,848 meters above sea level. Mauna Kea stands at a height of 4,205 meters above sea level, so that makes it shorter right?

Wrong.

Did you know, kids, that Mauna Kea, which juts out of the Pacific Ocean, is an old volcano that belongs to Hawaii? This volcanic mountain island formed over a million years ago when the tectonic plates moved on the ocean bed. So what you see is only half of the mountain jutting out of the ocean, the rest is located

below sea level, and if you measure the mountain from the ocean bed to its summit, it is an astounding 9,966 meters in height—move over Everest, Mauna Kea is the actually the tallest mountain on Earth (*Dickerson*, 2015).

Volcanoes in the ocean

 Volcanoes occur on land and on the ocean floor, but here's the best part kids: a volcano can even erupt under very cold ice caps! Volcanoes in the sea are called "submarine volcanoes," and almost two-thirds of the Earth's volcanoes are located under the sea.

The Story Of Brave Tilly Smith—The Girl Who Cried Tsunami!

I heard about the lovely Tilly Smith during my travels in England, and let me tell you about her amazing story of bravery and perception.

It was Boxing Day (December 26th) 2004, and young Tilly Smith, who was 10 years old, was on holiday in Thailand. That day the family was enjoying a warm, sunny morning walk on Mai Khao Beach on the island of Phuket.

Unnoticed by the rest of her family, Tilly saw the waves receding, getting dragged away from the shore, and there was froth on the sea just like when people pour a glass of beer. Tilly saw all that and remembered the geography class she had sat for just two weeks ago at school in England in which the children had been shown a movie about a tsunami that took place in Hawaii in 1946.

Hey, Tilly thought, *this beach in Thailand is behaving just like the beach in the movie.* Suddenly the little girl realized a tsunami was going to take place, and so she shouted for her family to leave the beach. Of course, her mom did not believe her, but eventually, her dad did and convinced the hotel staff to get people indoors.

And you know what? Just moments after that, a wave, nine meters tall, was seen speeding towards land. People just made it to the second floor of the hotel there and were saved. In fact, Mai Khao Beach had no casualties thanks to the brave actions of young Tilly.

Later, Tilly was presented with a Thomas Gray Special Award because she saved the lives of close to a hundred people. Isn't that just awesome? Tilly is the perfect example of paying attention to what you learn because you never know when important information can help you make a life-saving decision.

Wacky Weather Facts

Ever since I got hit by that bolt of lightning causing my brain to grow, I have been fascinated with the weather. It's quite alluring, scary, and fantastic all at the same time. Do you love thunderstorms, or do you prefer to hide under the duvet during one? I know a young pup who often heads straight under the bed every time a flash of lightning is followed by the rumble of thunder. Understanding how weather works is one way to stop being afraid of it. So, get ready to be blown away by these freaky weather facts I put together for you.

Sandstorms can cover an entire city!

 Sandstorms often occur in desert nations, also called the Middle East. However, countries like China experience sudden sandstorms, too. Some sandstorms can occur at heights of about 300 feet, swallowing up entire cities. All it takes is a few minutes for a sandstorm to cover everything in its path.

A mudslide is a very dangerous natural phenomenon that can carry away everything in its path

Including trees, rocks, houses, and vehicles. Mudslides, also called landslides, often occur after heavy rainfall when the placement of the slope gets disturbed and water veins from inside the slope cause parts of it to become dislodged and fall down. The entire face of a slope can slip down and obliterate anything in its path.

Your house will most likely be visited by more spiders the moment you start to experience mild autumn weather

This occurs because, as days get shorter, insects become more sensitive to the weather. Spiders are sensitive to changes in light and use it to gauge changing weather patterns. Therefore, shorter days and less light results in spiders getting ready for approaching winter by moving into your home to create a nice snug winter nest.

There is an old myth that says a bigger spider's web is an indication that autumn is approaching and temperatures are going to start dropping. While this myth is yet to be proven, entomologists do know this: A spider, like most bugs and humans, predicts weather patterns through light, but unlike us, many bugs have more than two eyes. There are two additional eyes located on the top of a spider's head called 'ocelli.' Through light, information is passed from these eyes to the spider's brain telling them that it's getting colder.

QUICK FACT

Who is an entomologist?

They are scientists who study arthropods. Some do it as a hobby and some as a career. Entomologists perform a very important job by studying the life cycles and habits of insects, arachnids, and other arthropods as they are very important for our planet.

A really bad heat wave can even cause rail tracks to bend.

It's true, kids. Traveling by train in extremely hot weather conditions can be dangerous because the heat can cause the train tracks to warp and bend. The heat causes the steel tracks to expand and turn into what I call spaghetti. And so, to ensure the safety of passengers, trains reduce their speeds when traveling in extremely hot weather, which can cause huge delays in schedules.

A bolt of lightning can be very hot

I know this is true because I got struck by a bolt of lightning! This phenomenon takes place because air cannot conduct heat properly and heats up very fast as soon as lightning passes through it. Researchers say the temperature of a lightning bolt can get up to 50,000 °F, which is hotter than the surface of the sun.

Our planet experiences about 2,000 thunderstorms every minute

No cause for alarm now, kids; these thunderstorms do not occur all in the same place. They are spread across the planet, which means that at any given moment a thunderstorm is taking place in many parts of the world.

Do you know how thunderstorms occur? What is called an 'unstable atmosphere' must take place for a thunderstorm to develop. Sudden differences in temperature and a convection current must take place for a thunderstorm to occur. Convection currents occur when large bodies of moist warm air that contain vaporized water make their way up into the atmosphere through a barrier of cold air. As the warm air makes its way up into the atmosphere, it creates pockets that get filled with more dense cold air. This combination of pressure causes storm clouds to form, resulting in thunderstorms.

A wildfire can create a fire tornado called a "fire whirl"

When a wildfire burns strong, it can create its own wind, which in turn causes the formation of tornadoes, or whirls of fire, which scientists call a fire whirl. They can be very tall and burn at a high temperature of about 1,994 °F.

Sometimes a miniature fire whirl can be seen in a bonfire or even a small fire, so next time you sit around camp make sure to look deep into the fire, and you may spot a mini fire whirl. Other names people use to describe a fire whirl are "fire tornado," "fire devil," and "fire twister." Pay attention to the news the next time you hear about a raging wildfire, you may just hear firefighters describing a fire whirl that is taking place. Pretty cool, right?

Next, let's explore the different continents of the Earth. My adventures across the world taught me so much about the cultures of our marvelous planet that I want to share the details with you. I've walked through rainforests, got chased by an angry ostrich on the plains of Africa, and met a very interesting Witch Doctor who wanted to make me his assistant. Let's learn about the people who live in faraway lands and their cultures and traditions, which are so different from what you may be used to at home.

Chapter 5: Exploring the Fascinating Continents of the World

The world is divided into seven continents, or areas that contain all the countries of the world. Due to the geographical location of each continent, there are differences in climate, environment, fauna, flora, and people. Each continent has unique differences in addition to the traditional cultures practiced within the countries located on those continents. To be an explorer and learn about the many differences on each continent is my dream.

Did you know that in the olden days' people believed

the world was flat and believed ships sailing to the edge of the Atlantic would fall off the Earth? That is until Christopher Columbus, from Spain on the European continent, discovered the North American continent and called it the New Land.

Are you ready to set off on an adventure across the seven continents with me? Let's start by recalling all seven continents of the world.

1. North America
2. South America
3. Africa
4. Europe
5. Asia
6. Australia
7. Antarctica

DID YOU KNOW?

The name 'America' comes from a very famous Italian navigator named Amerigo Vespucci?

He was one of the first explorers from Europe to travel to the New World, which is what the American continent was called right after its discovery by Christopher Columbus.

 At first, only the south was called America, but soon the entire landmass was given the name 'America,' then further dividing it into South America and North America.

THE SOUTH AMERICAN CONTINENT

The fourth largest of the world's continents, South America is a marvelous mix of cultures, and like Asia, is home to a very diverse population.

The people are friendly and love celebrations. The beaches are among the prettiest in the world while exploring the wilds is an exciting adventure with the Amazon River providing plenty of adventure as well as dangers to be aware of; the weather is warm and sunny, sometimes very sticky and hot, but it is all part of the adventure.

Since there are many nations located on this continent, there is an interesting diversity of cultures and food there. Many different languages and numerous old traditions and ancient tribes, like the Inca, make South America one of the world's most fascinating and exciting places to explore.

The culture in South America is very old and diverse. It is a vibrant mix of tribes that existed before Europeans arrived on the continent. The indigenous people, who are a beautiful mix of immigrants from Asia and Europe, as well as Africans brought over as slaves, have lent loads of colorful traditions and culture to the continent.

This diverse mix of cultures is reflected in many aspects. One of my favorites is the food. You can wander around South America tasting the variety of food, discovering new dishes in every country.

You will also see many cultural differences in the music, festivals, architecture, and religions of South America.

I have compiled a list of amazing facts about South America to help you understand the continent better.

Awesome Facts About South America

There are no doorbells in Paraguay

I once stood outside a friend's house in Paraguay in the pouring rain looking for a doorbell. There wasn't one, and I even tried barking, but no one answered the door! Do you know what I should have done?

I should have clapped! That's right, clapping a couple of times is a traditional way for visitors to announce they are at the door. You see kids, in Paraguay houses are located inside a compound surrounded by a wall and a gate. Visitors must never walk in, even if the gate is unlocked. They must clap for about 4–5 seconds to announce themselves.

South America is home to the world's longest mountain range

The Andes span a gigantic 4,350 miles from the north to the south of Latin America (another name for South America).

The Andes pass through seven countries: Peru, Venezuela, Bolivia, Ecuador, Argentina, Chile, and Colombia.

The average height of the mountain range is 4,000 meters.

There are a total of 12 countries on the continent but many languages are spoken!

South America is home to only 12 countries including Argentina, Bolivia, Brazil, Chile, Colombia, Ecuador, Guyana, Paraguay, Peru, Suriname, Uruguay, and Venezuela; however, over 400 languages are spoken there.

In South America, no one understands barking, except for the Latino dogs I met there. It's a good thing I understand human language because 450 languages have been recorded across the continent. This makes the South American continent the most linguistically diverse in the world.

• Portuguese and Spanish are the most commonly spoken languages on the continent.

• English, Italian, German, Arabic, Dutch, Japanese, Chinese, and Ukrainian are other languages spoken in

South America.

- There are many indigenous languages spoken on the continent. The most popular are Quechua, Guarani, and Aymara.
- The Quechua language was spread widely during the time of the Inca.

WHAT DOES 'LINGUISTICS' MEAN?

Linguistics is the study of human language, its evolution, and application.

Bolivia has no McDonald's.

Shocking as it sounds, Bolivia does not have any McDonald's outlets. However, there once were McDonald's restaurants in the country. The first was opened in La Paz in 1997. At the start, many people were excited about the arrival of McDonald's in Bolivia and formed long lines to get in.

In 2002, all branches were permanently closed down. There are several reasons. One is that people preferred local food over the Big Mac. This is because the preparation and consumption of food is almost sacred and a very hygienic practice with attention to every ingredient that goes into a meal. Unfortunately, McDonald's could not compete with this amazing love for food.

The world's highest-placed capital is in South America

La Paz, the capital of Bolivia, sits at an elevation of 3,650 meters. However, the title is not entirely clear because La Paz is classified as only the seat of the government, while the country's official capital status is awarded to the city of Sucre, which is located at only 2,810 meters.

The capital of Ecuador, Quito, located at an elevation of 2,850 meters, is the second-highest capital. (Or the first, when La Paz is not counted as the official capital.)

DID YOU KNOW?

Brazil is one of the most culturally diverse countries on the South American continent. The borders of Brazil are surrounded by 9 of the twelve countries in South America. Other than Ecuador and Chile, Brazil is surrounded by all other countries on the continent.

Gnocchi is eaten on the 29th of every month in Argentina

The tradition of eating gnocchi on the 29th day of every month started with the Italian immigrants who came to South America in the 19th century. According to tradition, money is placed under a plate of gnocchi as a symbol of good luck. Most restaurants in Argentina have special offers for all gnocchi dishes served on the 29th, so make sure to check out the menu if you do happen to head over to the country on your next vacation!

The Galapagos Islands in South America inspired Darwin to write his theory of evolution

What do you know about the amazing Galapagos Islands?

The islands are an archipelago located off the coast of sunny Ecuador, popular for its huge and diverse variety of animals and plant life thriving on land and in the sea. The wildlife in the Galapagos is amazing. There are over 500 species of fish and many unique endemic and endangered species. Every time I visit the islands, I feel overwhelmed by the diversity of wildlife and foliage, which makes this place one of the most marvelous natural environments in the world. Due to its special qualities, almost 97% of the islands are deemed a national park, and the surrounding sea is marked as a UNESCO Biosphere.

As you can see the world is quite an amazing and diverse place. There is so much more to learn.

FUN FACT

The island of Tristan da Cunha once accepted potatoes as money. Located in the South Atlantic, this island was located in such a remote quarter of the globe that people valued potatoes so much they used them as their unofficial currency.

NORTH AMERICA

This is the world's third-largest continent and is said to have been inhabited for over 30,000 years. The indigenous people of North America are the Native Americans, who lived there before the Europeans arrived. They consisted of over 500 tribes among which the Navajo, Cherokee, Sioux, Chippewa, Blackfeet, and Apache contributed the majority of the population.

After the discovery of the "New World" by Christopher Columbus in 1492, the European colonization of North America began, and the native tribes started to lose most of their homeland and were forced to live on reservations designated for them.

Today, North America is one of the world's most powerful nations, and despite many trials and wars—including the Civil War (1861-65), which was fought between the northern and southern regions of the United States in a bid to end slavery in the South—the nation has learned to live while respecting the rights and cultures of the various ethnicities that call the USA home.

Fun Facts from North America

Americans love pizza!

The nation eats about 100 acres of pizza a day on average, which amounts to a mind-boggling 350 slices every second! Well kids, in France we would say, "Bon Appetit! Enjoy your pizza!" (*Silly Facts*, 2015).

The Empire State Building is so big it has its own zip code

It's 10118, in case you want to send a letter to someone there. There are 2.8 million square feet offered for rent, and the building houses many prestigious offices such as LinkedIn and Shutterstock.

There is an observatory deck on the 102nd floor, and if you were to take the stairs you would have to climb 1,872 steps! Phew, I feel dizzy just thinking about it! But the good news is the building has over 70 elevators for a smooth ride to the top.

The largest national park on the continent is in Canada

Wood Buffalo National Park is 17,300 square miles (44,807 km²) and is bigger than Switzerland.

Mexico introduced the cacao bean to the world!

Boy, am I glad they did! In the olden days, the cacao bean was considered precious enough to be used as currency. The indigenous tribes used the bean to barter, while the Aztecs, who lived around Mexico before the Spanish took over in the 16th century, made a special but rather bitter cocoa drink which was reserved only for the Emperor. I'm sure glad I wasn't an Aztec emperor—I like my chocolate nice and sweet!

DID YOU KNOW?

Greenland is autonomous (an independent country), but it is listed as part of the North American continent and is also the largest island belonging to the continent. However, geopolitically, Greenland belongs to Europe because it is located in close proximity to the European continent. It is considered a part of the Kingdom of Denmark, although its range of autonomy is wide, and the classification does not include Greenland in Denmark's currency or foreign policies. The island has been populated by people from Europe and the Arctic area for over 5,000 years. That is one independent island, despite its location making it a part of different regions for different reasons.

THE AFRICAN CONTINENT

The second-largest continent in the world is Africa. If not for a very narrow strip of land in North Africa connecting the continent to Asia, Africa would be a totally independent mass of land. There are 48 countries and six island nations on the African continent.

QUICK FACT

Africa has many lures for visitors, including beautiful beaches and fascinating people, making it one of the world's most mysterious and charismatic continents, which was visited by many explorers in the past.

Africa's most famous explorer was Dr. David Livingston. He loved Africa so much that, though his body is buried in Westminster Abbey in England, his heart is buried in Africa under a beautiful Mvula tree!

What is Africa Famous For?

Africa is home to ancient cities and cultures

Africa is home to some of the world's oldest cultures and cities. Exploring places like Egypt and Morocco is a marvelous adventure full of mystery and exotic locales.

Do you know I once found a flying carpet in a dusty old shop in Morocco? Maybe it was the one used by Aladdin! Of course, you cannot find flying carpets in any of the shops in Africa today. Unless, of course, you are a genius bulldog with superpowers. If you love history and heritage, you should pay a visit to Morocco. The place is home to so many UNESCO World Heritage Sites that it is a treasure trove of wonders.

Top UNESCO Heritage Sites in Morocco

1. The Medina of Fez, founded in the 9th century, is home to the oldest university in the world.

2. The ancient city of Meknes, established in the 11th century, is a fascinating place to learn more about the Spanish and Moor influences in Morocco.

3. The Marrakesh Medina is home to many ancient mosques, palaces, and forts dating back to the 1070s when the medina was founded. Medina is a North African town surrounded by a wall.

Tribes and exotic cultures

Many tourists visit African tribes to see how the people live according to ancient traditions. Here are four of the most traditional African tribes you will find fascinating to learn about:

The Himba tribe living in northwest Namibia

You can identify the Himba from the color of their skin. It is a bright red from Otijize, the red ochre they rub on themselves as protection from the sun. The Himba are semi-nomadic, meaning they settle in one place for growing crops and travel only during particular seasons.

The Maasai people of Tanzania and Kenya

These people are known as warriors and will stay in one place only for a short time. The Maasai measure their wealth by the number of cattle a person owns.

The fascinating Zulu tribe of South Africa

Tthe largest of all South African ethnic groups and the most widely known tribe is famous for Shakaland, a replica of a traditional Zulu homestead known as a Umuzi.

It is a replica of the village of the world-famous Zulu chief, Shaka Zulu, who was born in the KwaZulu Natal Province. At Shakaland, you can learn more about the Zulu people, participate in their dances, and be a part of colorful traditional celebrations.

Colors and symbols are an important mode of communication amongst the tribes of Africa, especially the Zulu people. For example, the face paint that the tribes wear is in different shades of black, red, gray, purple, blue, and more.

Purple symbolizes royalty, while black indicates evil and mystery, often worn by the witch doctors. Symbols are used to tell a story and are an indication of a tribal family's history; the symbols serve as reminders of the trials, triumphs, and bravery those families have been through.

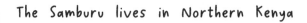

The Samburu lives in Northern Kenya

This tribe is known as one of the friendliest. They are connected to the Massai but still retain their traditional dress and way of life, tending to livestock as their main income. They are unlike the Maasai who have become more modernized by adopting a more westernized type of dress and seeking employment outside of their homestead.

AFRICA AND IT'S NATURAL WONDERS

The beautiful geographical location of Africa has blessed the continent with many natural wonders. I was quite stunned to see how beautiful this huge continent was. Some of the beautiful sights I saw were:

- the world's largest land animal – the African elephant. It can only be found in the African continent
- four of the world's fastest land animals: cheetah, wildebeest, Thomson's gazelle, lion
- the oldest desert in the world - the Namib desert. It is home to the tallest sand dunes in the world

- the longest river in the world—the Nile

- the world's biggest waterfall - Victoria Falls

- the third-largest desert - the Sahara

- the world's second-largest river canyon - Fish River Canyon (the first being the Grand Canyon in the US)

- the largest inland delta in the world—the Okavango Delta

QUICK FACTS FROM AFRICA

1. Coffee was first discovered by Kaldi (850 CE), an Ethiopian goat herder who noticed how frisky and unwilling to sleep at night his goats became after eating the berries from a certain tree. Kaldi brand coffee is world-famous.

2. A year lasts 13 months in Ethiopia. The first 12 months have 30 days, while the 13th month has only 5 days, or 6 every leap year.

3. Sudan is home to more pyramids than Egypt. Sudan has over 200 pyramids, while Egypt has 138.

4. An average Rashaida household in Sudan owns between 50-70 camels. They are considered important important assets serving as food, transport, and also pets in Rashaida households.

5. The hottest country in the world is Mali in West Africa.

EUROPEAN CONTINENT

There are 44 countries on the European continent, home to some very fascinating and diverse nations. Since cultures and traditions among the nations of Europe are so diverse, I thought you could learn a bit about the nations through these interesting facts I have lined up for you kids—enjoy!

It is bad luck to wish someone "happy birthday" in advance, according to an old German superstition!

Yikes, I'm glad I found that out before I visited my friend Axle for his birthday!

Oh, and one more from Germany: cover your mouth when you yawn, or else a demon may invade your soul.

In Greece, most old structures are painted in a brilliant turquoise-blue, do you know why?

The Greeks believe the color keeps away the evil eye.

In Greece, do not wave with your palm facing the person with your finger spread as this gesture is considered an insult

Well, to be on the safe side, all I do is wag my tail hello and goodbye.

Did you know the most popular and most visited place in Europe is the Louvre Museum in Paris?

 Yes, and it is home to the Mona Lisa, a beautiful and famous painting by Leonardo Da Vinci, an Italian artist.

QUICK FACT

The smallest country in the world is Vatican City. It is located within the city of Rome in Italy. It is an independent city-state.

Do you know where the most chocolate is sold?

Chocolate

At the Brussels Airport in Belgium, of course, because Belgian chocolate is so fine. Over 800 tons of it is sold every year.

Lawn mowing on Sunday is against the law in Switzerland

If you were in Switzerland, and your mom asked you to mow the lawn on a Sunday, you could say, "Nope, Mom, it's illegal." Lawn mowing on Sunday is against the law, so is washing clothes and hanging them out to dry, washing your car, and even trying to build anything. This is because Sunday is a day of rest, and no one wants noisy neighbors mowing lawns. Now that's where I want to be on Sunday—chilling on a lovely green lawn with a big glass of lemonade.

FUN FOOD FACTS FROM EUROPE

The French fry is from Belgium, not France. Historians have found evidence to show that people in Belgium were frying potatoes in the 1600s. The trend started when villagers in a place called Meuse Valley started slicing and frying potatoes when they could no longer fish during the winter months.

Did you know that American soldiers who were stationed in Belgium ate French fries for the first time while there? And kids, I must tell you that the only French Fry Museum in the world is located in Belgium. It is called the Frietmuseum—check it out online! By the way, there still is quite a dispute among the French and Belgians as to who actually invented the delicious French fry!

AUSTRALIA – THE LAND DOWN UNDER

The Australian continent is the only one that's home to a single country—Australia! It is one of the more fascinating continents on our planet, home to diverse landscapes and really odd animals, called 'critters' by the locals.

English is the official language, although Australians have their own lingo for certain words!

Let's check some out for the next time you visit the continent and want to say more than "Good day, mate!"

1. cake hole—mouth; makes sense kids, because what better way to remember mouth than cake!

2. Sheila—a woman

3. bush telly—is not really about watching a traditional television; it is actually enjoying your surroundings as you camp: the vast open sky, the stars, the surrounding bush, and the campfire

4. roo—kangaroo; watch out, those hoppy guys are all over the place

5. bikki—biscuit

If you think Australians talk funny, check out these interesting facts.

There are more kangaroos in Australia than humans

According to a 2019 survey by the Australian Government, there are 50 million kangaroos and only 25 million people (Kangaroos, 2019).

The banknotes in Australia are resistant to moisture

They are waterproof and much cleaner in comparison to those from other nations. Oh, and they are harder to counterfeit.

The indigenous people of Australia are called Aboriginals

DNA studies have shown they are one of the world's oldest known civilizations. Their ancestry goes back 75,000 years.

Aboriginal art is beautiful and unique; the pictures are created through a system of colorful dots.

A didgeridoo is a traditional Aboriginal wind instrument that's like a long pipe and is considered a very sacred item. You must first get permission from your Aboriginal friend before using one.

The land of the Kiwi, which we better know as New Zealand, located next to the Australian continent, is totally beautiful. Located on the South Pacific Ocean, New Zealand is a part of Oceania.

When I visited, I could see there were lots of sheep. So I asked around, counted, and found out that in New Zealand there are more sheep than people. In fact, the ratio is five to six sheep for every one person when last counted in January 2019 (*Joe*, 2021). I wonder if there are vacancies for sheepdogs?

ANTARCTICA

Kids, I visited this continent, and let me tell you it was the coldest, windiest continent on Earth. And it's huge, covering an area of 5.5 million square miles (14.2 million km²).

Soon after I started exploring, there were icicles forming on my whiskers and I had to stop for a hot chocolate near a group of very friendly penguins who invited me to go swimming with them. I said no, of course, because I did not want to freeze my tail off!

Want to go for a swim?

Antarctica can be classified as a "polar desert"

 No, not because it's hot and sandy; on the contrary, it is cold and covered in ice. But what we call a 'desert' is land that receives minimal precipitation (snow, rainfall, fog, mist), and Antarctica receives very little snowfall and rain—the annual average precipitation there is two inches of rain or snow (*Gallo*, 2021).

The continent is also home to the largest collection of freshwater on the planet

The water is held as a very thick sheet of ice that took millions of years to form.

Hardly any plants or trees grow there

In fact, only two varieties of flowering plants, the Antarctica Pearlwort and Antarctica Hair grass, are found along with a lot of moss, fungi, and algae that thrive on the icy continent.

The fishes in Antarctica are really special

 They stop themselves from freezing in the icy cold water with a type of protein in their blood that prevents them from freezing up.

Time is not proper in Antarctica because all the world's different time zones meet at a point on the South Pole

 Night and day are pretty bizarre too. In summertime, the continent has six months of endless sunlight, and then six months of darkness in winter.

DID YOU KNOW?

The South Pole is much colder than the North Pole!

 This is because the South Pole is located on a very thick layer of ice, which, in turn, is located on the continent. The elevation of this ice sheet is a whopping 9,000 feet, which, if measured from sea level, is over a mile and a half high.

ASIA

The Asian continent consists of many countries as it is the biggest in the world. There are 48 countries and three territories in Asia, making it a wonderfully colorful land of different people following customs and traditions handed down over many generations.

Russia makes up a major portion of the Asian continent, but only 22% of Russia's population lives there. And so, Russia is not counted as one of the countries in Asia; if it was, the number would go up to 49%.

Cultural Customs in Asia

Greetings are different in each region

A handshake, although common in Western countries, is not the traditional way to greet someone in Asia.

In Japan, China, and South Korea, people greet each other with a slight bow with their hands by the sides of their body.

In Thailand, India, and Sri Lanka, people will bring their hands together in a prayer position and say hello with a slight nod of the head. This type of greeting will be followed by a phrase in their native language. In India, people say *namaste*, while in Sri Lanka they would say *ayubowan* (a-yu-bo-wan). In Thailand, this greeting is called the *wai*. The people say *sawadee krab/ka*, meaning "hello!" And it is said with a big smile. Generally, a man would end the sentence with *krab* and a woman with *ka*.

Taking off shoes before entering a home

It is a tradition in most Asian homes for visitors to remove their shoes before entering a person's home, or a shrine. This custom is practiced in China, Thailand, Japan, South Korea, and other Asian nations. Shoes are also removed before entering a Buddhist temple or a Hindu Kovil.

Festivals, Food, Customs, and Seasonal Celebrations in Asia

During all my travels, I was most impressed with how different and vibrant cultures across the world are. There are so many wonderful traditions and celebrations to be a part of that make traveling a very enjoyable experience. For example, if you were to visit the sunny island of Sri Lanka, you would learn that the people there celebrate the dawn of a New Year in the month of April, not January 1st as we do. Here are some famous celebrations you will probably want to learn more about, or even tell your parents about so they can plan your next vacation to coincide with one!

The Dragon Boat Festival in Singapore

Singapore is a small country located in Southeast Asia. It is home to many ethnic races such as the Chinese, Malays, and Indians. Singapore is a beautiful and colorful nation where you can be a part of fabulous celebrations all year round.

In summer, Singapore celebrates the Dragon Boat Festival together with other Southeast Asian countries. During this festival, boats are built and painted to look like fierce and colorful dragons. They are then entered into very exciting races.

The competition is a tradition in many Southeast Asian countries, and eating delicious sticky rice dumplings is also a part of these summer celebrations. The race is a popular sport and has been a part of Chinese culture for over 2,000 years. The festival is a fun and happy traditional celebration that brings people together.

Songkran in Thailand

Thailand is a country in Southeast Asia. It is a nation with a very old culture, and people still follow many cultural traditions linked to Buddhism. Bangkok is the capital of Thailand and is a very popular holiday destination for shopping and eating delicious street food.

Songkran is one of the most popular Buddhist water festivals in Thailand where people enjoy loads of fun on the streets. The festival signals the start of the New Year according to the Buddhist calendar and is held on April 13th each year.

I visited Thailand during this time with kids, and

boy, did I have loads of fun! Everyone is out on the streets with water cannons and buckets of water, and anyone caught outside gets doused. It's all in good fun and even tourists enjoy the festival.

People visit their hometowns and spend time praying in the temples during Songkran. The Buddha statues, too, are washed with water as a symbol of the festivities signaling new beginnings.

Now let me tell you that Thailand is one of the best places for a foodie like me, and during Songkran you can sample a variety of popular Thai food. Here is my favorite:

Mango Sticky Rice

Sticky rice is an all-time favorite dessert in Thailand. The rice is cooked in creamy coconut cream and served with slices of fresh mango.

QUICK FACT ON THAI EATING HABITS

In Thailand, people do not use chopsticks like in China or Singapore; they prefer using a fork and spoon. Also, it is considered rude to put the fork in your mouth. Instead, it is used to push food onto the spoon.

You can eat with your hand, but only your right hand, as in most Asian cultures the left hand is considered unclean. Do not touch food with your palm; use only the tips of your fingers to pick up and eat food. Eating sticky rice with your hand is the best.

Festival of Spring-Holi, India

India is located in South Asia and is a vibrant country with many traditions, cultures, and religions. Indian food is popular across the world. My favorite is Palak Paneer. The people there celebrate several festivities linked to religion.

Holi, the festival of colors, is a popular Hindu festival celebrated in India. It is a celebration of love. According to legend, Lord Krishna loved a girl called Radha, but Krishna had unusually colored skin (he is depicted with blue-colored skin). Krishna feared Radha would not like his dark color and asked her to color his skin with any color she liked. This she did, and the two ended up falling in love.

Holi celebrates the coloring of Krishna by Radha, and the entire nation of India explodes in a kaleidoscope of colors as people take special colored powders that are safe to use and throw them at each other. Just like Songkran the water festival, Holi has people throwing colored powder, and everyone soon starts to look like walking rainbows. During Holi, Hindus spend time engaged in holy rituals at the kovil (the Hindu temple), giving thanks to God Krishna, who is considered the creator of the Universe.

Holi is celebrated in March, but the specific day changes based on the moon's cycles. On the first evening of the full moon, Holika Dahan is celebrated by lighting large bonfires to represent the burning of the demon *Holika*, symbolizing the triumph of good over evil. The next day, Rangwali Holi is celebrated with a splash of color and loads of fun on the streets. There are many delicious dishes to try during the Holi festival.

126

Gujiya

This is a heavenly sweet treat I absolutely love. They are made with crisp and flaky pastry stuffed with nuts, raisins, and palm sugar called jaggery. The pastry is put into a golden sweet sugar syrup before being eaten—yum!

Mid-Autumn Festival in Hong Kong

Hong Kong was under the rule of the British until 1997, after which it became a part of China once more. The Mid-Autumn Festival celebrated in Hong Kong is a very colorful and wild affair that traditionally includes eating mooncakes and lighting colorful lanterns.

Today, an exciting part of the festival is the parade of a giant Fire Dragon; it's 67 meters long and carried across Tai Hang in Causeway Bay. The dragon is made up of tens of thousands of incense sticks woven into hemp rope to create a spine and a rattan frame head around which pearl straw is coiled to accommodate the incense sticks. The dragon is then held up and walked across the streets by close to 300 men to the sound of cheers and happy celebrations.

Traditional food eaten at the Mid-Autumn Festival

This festival coincided with the harvest festival in China in the olden days. The Mid-Autumn Harvest Festival is a fabulous celebration with delicious traditional food.

Mooncakes

This is by far the most important of all festival foods. As the time draws near for the Mid-Autumn Festival, you will notice a variety of mooncakes are sold in Asian stores in your neighborhood. Mooncakes are really a type of pastry inside which a delicious sweet filling is found. Traditionally, this filling consists of sweet bean paste, lotus seeds, and egg yolks, but I have found several variations which I simply love, such as the yummy chocolate mooncakes.

Here's a fun fact about mooncakes I learned, kids: It is believed that mooncakes were used by Han Chinese revolutionaries to send messages to each other during the terrible reign of the Mongolians. The story goes that the Han people were prohibited from gathering in groups and had no way of discussing their plans to defeat the cruel Mongols, so they used mooncakes to smuggle messages. On the night of the Moon Festival, hundreds of mooncakes with instructions to rebel were sent to the Chinese people who, upon reading them, attacked the Mongolians and secured victory and freedom.

In Singapore, mooncakes are filled with durian, a tropical fruit that is considered a delicacy in Asian countries. But do you know, kids, that durian, loved by many for being a superfood packed with nutrients, has a very strong smell. And so, some hotels and even public transport in Malaysia and Singapore ban guests from entering with the fruit.

Some Unusual Facts From Asia

Here are some quirky facts from Asia you may find interesting.

Why the left hand is considered unclean

The left hand is considered unclean in many Asian cultures in countries such as India, Thailand, Nepal, Bangladesh, Pakistan, Maldives, Sri Lanka, and in parts of the Middle East. This is because in ancient times these cultures revered their dominant hand, which was usually the right hand, and so it was established as the hand that should be used for eating, cooking, writing, and so forth.

The left hand was used for sanitary purposes such as washing oneself after using the toilet. Therefore, the left hand was considered the 'unclean' hand and still is by most Asian cultures.

Vending machines are a dime a dozen in Japan

We all love Japan for its amazing inventions designed to make life super easy and interesting. Well, did you know that Japan has the highest number of vending machines? There is one for every 30 people statistically speaking.

Here is a list of some really weird stuff sold from vending machines in Japan:

Live bugs. They are kept alive and well in special containers for anyone needing to study them. The dwindling environmental reserves making it harder to find bugs to study led to this rather odd vending machine sale.

Neckties. You know how sometimes a person could be really enjoying a bowl of Ramen to suddenly find his tie soaked in the soup? Well, in Japan it's not a problem, all you do is hop over to the nearest vending machine selling ties and choose the one you want!

Eggs. Yes, eggs are sold in vending machines. So those Japanese hens sure have their work cut out making enough eggs to fill all those machines.

Pizza. Oh, yes I love this idea! You simply pop in a few coins, and you've got a pizza on the way. Don't you think that banana pie vending machines would be a great hit too?

Bug snacks. I know some of you will love this. Imagine asking your mom for money to get snacks, and you hit the machine for a pack of bug snacks! In Japan you can, and they are crispy and delicious.

Taiwan, garbage, and Beethoven

What's the connection, you wonder? Well, in Taiwan people hear the sound of Beethoven's "Für Elise" at the sight of a big yellow garbage truck; that's the signal to take their garbage to the curb to be picked up. Classical music and dump trucks—what a combination!

Next, we delve into one of my favorite subjects—history. Ever since I invented my time machine, I have been having so much fun zipping back and forth through time. I even managed to stamp my name, "Ronny the Frenchie," on a pyramid in Egypt as it was being built!

130

Chapter 6: World History

Lost cities, ancient civilizations, fierce battles, mighty kingdoms, ruthless kings and queens, and battles for freedom are just a few of the factors that make world history an amazing subject to learn about.

I used my time traveling machine to go back to the past and meet up with some very interesting people. I learned about mighty kingdoms before they fell and became forgotten ruins, I met famous people from the past and learned more about their struggles and accomplishments, and I have compiled the coolest facts from all my journeys back to the past for you to learn and be amazed.

Ancient Egypt—Some Interesting Trivia

Come on my young explorers, grab on to my tail and let's swing back 5,000 years to look at the start of Egypt and its journey throughout the years.

The pyramids

There are over 130 pyramids that have been discovered up to now in Egypt. Did you know that pyramids are actually giant tombs for the pharaohs (kings) of Egypt? They were buried there with vast treasures that their family thought they would need to start their new life in the afterworld.

Egyptian laborers organized strikes

You must understand that building those pyramids was no easy task, and on occasion, ancient Egyptian workers were known to organize strikes. They knew their rights and were not afraid to protest if they were treated unjustly. One of the earliest recorded strikes was held in Egypt during the reign of Ramses III in the 12 century BC.

The afterlife

The afterlife for Egyptians was the next step. They believed that once a person died, they moved on to the next world (the afterlife), and so the dead were mummified, and their bodies and internal organs preserved so they could wake up whole in the afterlife. Royalty was always buried with lots of treasure to make sure they had plenty of everything when they moved onto the underworld.

Here's a funny fact - the pharaohs were fat

According to scientists who examined the mummies of Egyptian Pharaohs and Queens, they believe most were overweight and suffered from diabetes. It is believed the royal diet of beer, bread, and honey contributed to the weight gain. Queen Hatshepsut is a fine example of being the opposite to the slim figure shown on her coffin cover (*Small,* 2007).

Have you heard of "Wepet Renpet"?

No, it's not the name of a Kleenex brand! Wepet Renpet actually means New Year in ancient Egypt. Directly translated, the words mean "the opening of the New Year." This new year was not celebrated on January 1st, oh no! Wepet Renpet happens on different days every year. The ancient Egyptians celebrated this new year's festival to coincide with the flooding of the Nile River. Therefore, to predict the day for Wepet Renpet, astrologers would study the night sky for about 70 days after the brightest star in the sky, Sirius, disappeared. The reappearance of Sirius in the sky predicted the Nile would soon flood and it was time to celebrate the New Year festival, which lasted for many days and included lots of dancing, eating, and celebrations.

Hieroglyphs

The alphabet of the ancient Egyptians is called 'hieroglyphs.' It was not

 made up of letters like our alphabet but consisted of pictures, or rather, symbols. There are 700 hieroglyphs that the ancient Egyptians used to communicate. Each one of the symbols has a meaning, and archaeologists have learned to read them.

Cats were considered good luck

Although I don't see the reason behind the ancient Egyptians considering cats to be sacred, it's true. Almost every household had a pet cat that was treated like royalty simply because they thought the feline would bring them good luck. Of course, dogs were respected, as I told you in a previous chapter because we were considered friends and lifelong companions, even being mummified to make the journey to the afterlife to be with our masters.

Let's not forget that Anubis, the god of the underworld, is often shown with a jackal's head, so people often identified their dogs with the god.

Ancient Egyptians were responsible for many inventions we still use

Well, apart from thinking cats were sacred, ancient Egyptians were very smart and came up with inventions that we still use today.

1. Reed pens made from cut sticks of bamboo or bullrush are amongst the oldest writing instruments.

2. Paper called Papyrus made from the stem of the papyrus plant is still produced today.

3. Locks and keys made from wood that unlocked pins inside a bolt were shaped like your toothbrush.

4. Sundials were first invented in Egypt and Babylon. The oldest ever found is from Egypt dating back to 1,500 BC. The Obelisk, a huge rock column, was the first type of sundial built by the Egyptians. They told time judging by the shadow cast from the huge rock.

QUICK FACT

Senet, the ancient board game is originated in Egypt. The game is over 2,000 years old and is still played today.

Ancient Greece

Greece was a fascinating nation in the olden days and was not the peaceful idyllic place it is today. There were many fierce battles fought, mighty rulers who dominated the world, and worship of many gods and goddesses to whom the Greeks built huge monuments. Greeks loved arts and culture.

Alexander the Great

Alexander the Great was born in 356 BC, and died in 323 BC, at the young age of 32. He was a mighty Greek ruler who accomplished much in his short life span. Alexander III came from a place called Macedon in Greece. He is famous for conquering most of western Asia and northeast Africa and ruled over a huge army that marched across the lands.

> Just like Alexander the Great, life expectancy in Greece was low. Women lived an average of 36 years, and men 45. Did you know that a six-year-old dog would be 40 in human years?

The greatest battle in Greek history is the battle of Thermopylae

The Greeks fought the Persian army, of which historians estimate may have exceeded 300,000. With only 7,000 soldiers on their side, the

Greeks were led by a brave leader called Leonidas who, even after being outnumbered, stood his ground with a small army to triumph against the mighty Persians.

The Greeks worshiped many gods, and the gods in turn ruled over lesser (demi) gods

There were 12 head gods known as the Olympian Gods, who people believed lived on Mount Olympus.

The most prominent Greek gods were Zeus, the head, Poseidon, who ruled the seas, and Hera, wife of Zeus and goddess who ruled over women.

Ancient Rome

The Roman civilization, which was founded in the 8th century, is what we call ancient Rome. In the 5th century AD, what was known as the Western Roman Empire fell. What began as a little town close to the Tiber River in Italy became a mighty empire conquering many lands.

The historical Trajan's Market in Rome was a mall

Constructed between 100–110 AD, it is believed to have been the first shopping mall-like complex there and housed shops and offices.

 Romans believed that if you see an owl, it's bad luck, but spotting a bee is good luck.

Romans made a big deal of baths and had them in special complexes

Kind of like our indoor pools, the wealthy citizens of Rome attended their Roman Baths with a battalion of slaves who carried their clothes, sandals, and scented oils. They did not, however, use soap.

There were female gladiators in ancient Rome

 That's right, it wasn't only huge muscly men who fought in the arena. There were brave women gladiators too; they were called Gladiatrices or Gladiatrix (sounds almost like someone from Asterix). The women warriors fought against each other, and sometimes animals.

The Mayan Kingdom

The ancient Mayans were a mighty kingdom. They built many great cities (almost 60) and were very prosperous and feared by most other civilizations.

They lived in Mesoamerica which belonged to areas around Central America and Mexico.

Mayans were smart and invented many things

Smart cultivation systems, the Mayan calendar systems, games and sports as well as systems for writing such as glyphic cartouche, which is similar to words and sentence structures we use today.

Mayans showed their status through their love of hats

The more important the person was, the bigger their headdresses.

The Mayans worshiped the elements and had many gods

The Mayans worshiped gods such as the god of rain, god of sun, of storms, the night, the moon and the creator of the universe. They also thought turkeys were gods and worshiped them. They believed that turkeys possessed magical powers and that they could use them to harm the Maya when they were in a dream state. And so the turkey was feared and respected.

Important Facts About the Great and Devastating World War II

The most devastating war in human history was World War II (WWII). Starting September 1, 1939, the war raged for six years and came to an end on September 2, 1945. Here are some points on WWII you must know as they are a very important set of events that shaped the world. WWII was fought between the Allies and the Axis.

The Allies and the Axis

The Allied powers were made up of Britain, the USA, France, the Soviet Union, and China while Germany, Italy, and Japan were called the Axis forces. Germany was led by a man named Adolph Hitler.

Brave women manufacture many marvelous things

With most of the men off fighting and countries using all their finances to fund the war, a lot of factories were shut down, but some were run by the brave women who took the place of their fathers, brothers, and husbands to manufacture many marvelous things including airplanes. Close to 310,000 women were recruited into the US aircraft industry by 1943 (*History.com*

Editors, 2021).

Almost 60 million people died as a result of WWII

This sad fact remains as a reminder to us all that there are no winners in war, and striving to arrive at peaceful solutions to problems is always the best tactic.

The United Nations (UN), an international organization with the goal to protect international peace

The UN was formed with 51 member countries in 1945 after WWII ended. The purpose of the organization was to maintain world peace and security, develop friendly ties between countries, and the promotion of human rights, higher standards of living, and social progress.

African-American Civil Rights Activists in the US

The civil rights all people in the US enjoy today were achieved due to the tireless work, struggles, and endless battles fought by remarkable individuals who were brave enough to stand up against the discrimination of the African-American community in the past.

While citizens of the US enjoy equal rights today, regardless of race, it was not always that way. The African slaves who fought hard for their freedom faced a lot of discrimination and had no proper rights within the community. It was a long and hard battle fought by many, including the people listed below. They are responsible for winning you the rights and equality in society you enjoy today.

W.E.B. Du Bois

 A leading intellectual amongst the colored community at the time, Du Bois is the founder of the NAACP, which stands for the National Association for the Advancement of Colored People. Formed in 1909, the goal of the organization was to obtain equality and justice for the African-Americans in the US. Du Bois was the author of several books that described how the Black community was treated. He was also responsible for empowering the African-American community to embrace their proud African heritage despite being citizens of the US.

Thurgood Marshall

The first Black Supreme Court Justice in the US, Marshall legally fought against the segregation of the African-American community.

Rosa Parks

This brave woman is an icon for the Black rights movement in the US. In case you didn't know, kids, before civil rights were established for the African-American people, there were some very odd rules that people had to follow.

The seating in buses, for example, was separate with the first few rows being reserved for white people and the latter rows for colored people.

In 1955, on a bus in Montgomery, Alabama, Rosa Parks made history when she refused to give up her seat in the "Black section" and move to the back because the driver wanted to make more  room for the white people since the "White section" was full. If I was with Rosa then, I sure would have nipped the heels of anyone who tried to take her seat.

Rosa was brave, though, and stood her ground. Her actions sparked a very successful boycott of buses by the people of Montgomery. Avoiding buses, people started to carpool, take taxis, and even walk; I walked beside some of the people on their way to work and found out some of them walked close to 20 miles. But no one complained because they were fighting for a very important cause.

Do you know who it was that initiated the boycott, as the newest Black rights activist in Montgomery? It was none other than Martin Luther King, Jr!

 The segregation of people on buses was put to a stop in 1956, when a Supreme Court order was passed stating the act as unconstitutional.

*Unconstitutional—an act that violates a person's or group of people's constitutional rights.

※·※·※·※·※·※·※·※·※·※·※·※·※·※·※

FUN FACTS

Rosa Parks wrote her autobiography, *Rosa Parks, My Story*, in 1992.

Parks received the Presidential Medal of Freedom in 1996.

Rosa was the first woman to lay in honor at the United States Capitol Rotunda in Washington DC when she died. Her casket was kept at the Rotunda for two days for public viewing. She died in 2005 at the age of 92 and is buried at Woodlawn Cemetery in Detroit.

Rosa's full-length statue, commissioned by Congress, was the first of an African-American to be placed in the capital of the US.

The Capitol Rotunda is located under the Capitol Dome; the complex that marks the physical heart (center) of Washington, DC.

※·※·※·※·※·※·※·※·※·※·※·※·※·※·※

Quirky History Facts

Here are some very interesting tidbits on history I think you guys will find quite interesting.

The first person to circumnavigate the globe

Portuguese explorer Ferdinand Magellan initiated the very first circumnavigation of the globe between 1519 and 1522. He set sail on a commission by the King of Spain and set off on a quest to find an easy route to the Orient. He sailed towards the west from the southern tip of the American continent. The strait at the southernmost tip of the South American continent was found by Magellan who named it "Channel of All Saints," and although the name changed over the years, the channel remains dedicated to the man who found it. You may know it as the Strait of Magellan. Once Magellan crossed the choppy water of the strait, his ship emerged onto a very calm ocean, and you know what he named that ocean? He called it the Pacific Ocean.

Sadly, Magellan died before he could complete the entire journey, and it was Juan Sebastian del Cano who completed the course mapped out by Magellan.

Vikings were trendsetters

Do you have images of strong, fierce warriors when you think about the Vikings? Well, they were, but they were also very conscious about their image. The men would often dye their hair blonde, which was considered the best hair color. They even dyed their beards, used an ear spoon to clean out their ears, and were said to take more baths than most people did at the time. The Vikings, like most of the European communities at the time, were trendsetters. Now isn't that an amazing fact?

The making of the world's first cartoon

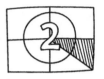

Ah, cartoons, how I love them, especially classics like Scooby-Doo. But kids, do you know who created the very first cartoon? It was a Frenchman from my home country named Emile Cohl. He created the cartoon "*Fantasmagorie*," which consisted of 700 drawings and ran for just two minutes. Still, it was a start, and we all know how far animation, or cartoons, have come today. The short film was released on August 17, 1908. And you know what? If you search on YouTube for "*Fantasmagorie*," you can watch the world's very first cartoon!

75-200 million people died in Europe and North Africa because of rats

Sounds terrible? It was, but not in the horrific rats-eating-people kind of scenario you might be imagining right now.

The Bubonic Plague, better known as the Black Death, is a deadly disease that spreads from fleas and rats to humans. A quarter of the population in Europe died from the Black Death between 1347 and 1351. One of the most devastating plagues faced by the world, the Black Death created a huge impact on the course of European history.

Ohaguro: Teeth blackening

In ancient Japan during the Heian period from 794 to 1185 AD, women would dye their teeth black, simply because they considered white unattractive. However, this tradition was banned by the Meiji government in 1870.

Did you know King Louis XIX was king of France for only 20 minutes?

His father, Charles X, was forced to abdicate the throne in 1830 due to public protest, but Louis Antoine, who took over as King Louis XIX, had to abdicate too due to the same protests.

Pineapple was a symbol of status in England around the 18th century

Do you think the upper class went around carrying a pineapple in their hands? Well, some people actually did carry one around as a symbol of prosperity, but mostly they were added to decorations in the middle of dinner tables to impress guests. No one ate it because it was considered almost sacred. And so, pineapples were sometimes rented whenever someone had a party and wanted to impress their guests.

Chapter 7: Sports & Leisure

The world of sports is truly fascinating. We all love watching or playing our favorite game.

I personally love a game of frisbee, or even football, with my human friend. Especially at the beach on a warm summer day.

I love baseball, too, but more because of all the free hot dogs I get from people around who think I look very cute sitting there with my old Red Sox cap on my head. I'm not really a fan, but I was given the cap by a friend, so I wear it whenever I go to games where the Red Sox are playing. Maybe you have heard of my friend; I met Babe Ruth the last time I traveled back in time in my time machine.

 Are you into a sport?

If you are, you know how much  dedication goes into achieving dreams and goals in a chosen sport. It is a lot of hard work that empowers many watching and taking part in the sport.

 Do you remember how exciting a Little League Baseball game can get, or how much you cheer your friends on when they are racing on the track?

Well, that is the thrill of sport that we all enjoy.

Basketball, football, and cricket are sports loved across the world with millions of fans. There are also lesser-known sports and learning about them will certainly make you go "wow!"

Fascinating and Crazy Sports Facts

Olympic snowboarders

Did you know that a snowboarder competing in the Olympics will soar about 46 feet in the air? That's about as high as a building with four floors. Snowboarding has been a part of the Winter Olympics for more than 20 years. It is quite similar to regular vert skateboarding events and takes place inside an enormous half-pipe that has vertical walls.

Soccer is all about distance

Is Cristiano Ronaldo your favorite soccer player? I have often tried to imitate his cool moves. Well, here is a cool fact about soccer I recently learned: During a full match, a midfielder will run a total of about seven miles, but the referee will run even more! So the next time you watch a match, keep your eye on the ref and see how much exercise he gets running behind the players.

FUN FACT!

Soccer is a Medieval game.

If you were to travel to Britain, people there would talk about 'football' instead of 'soccer' because while it means the same sport, in the US we call it soccer.

The word 'soccer' developed from a slang term for Association Football and has a history of over 100 years in Britain itself.

A term used in Britain, Association Football, which is a football league, was shortened by players who called it soccer.

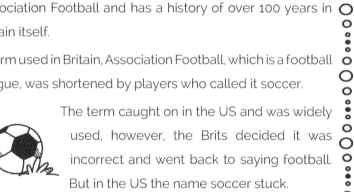

The term caught on in the US and was widely used, however, the Brits decided it was incorrect and went back to saying football. But in the US the name soccer stuck.

Lefties may have better luck at sports

In baseball, tennis, fencing, and even boxing, around 20–30% of the best athletes are left-handed. Being left-handed in sports is kind of like having a superpower because while around 90% of people are right-handed, a leftie is unique and can use their uncommon lefty advantage in sports (*Ferocious Media*, 2019).

Being left-handed can be advantageous in returning the ball in tennis, pitching in baseball, and even contact sports like boxing. The right-handed opponent gets thrown off-guard with that left-sided punch or return.

Some top left-handed sportsmen include Babe Ruth, Rafael Nadal, Manu Ginobili, Monica Seles, Michael Redd, and many more.

Are you a leftie who is taking part in a sport? Well, go use your superpower to your advantage!

The world's oldest sport

Wrestling is believed to be one of the oldest sports. It first took place in Greece around 776 BC.

Black undies for all Major League Baseball umpires

Okay kids, I am still rolling around laughing at this one, but it's true. All umpires of Major League games must wear black underwear. It's a safety measure in case their pants happen to split open. Umpires at Major League Baseball games are given the highest standard of respect, and no player can go above an umpire's decision. Therefore, to save them any embarrassment, it is a requirement to wear black undies.

The Olympic flag

Designed in 1912 by Baron Pierre de Coubertin, known as the "Father of the Olympics," the five rings on the Olympic flag represent the five continents from which athletes come to perform at the games.

Did you also know that the colors of the rings against the white background were specifically chosen to represent the color of every national flag in existence at the time the Olympic flag made its debut in 1914? Well, it was!

Michael Phelps has won more gold medals than whole nations

American swimmer Michael Phelps has won more gold medals than some entire nations such as Mexico and Portugal going all the way back to 1896. Phelps won five gold medals and one silver during his amazing performance at the 2016 Olympics in Rio.

His entire collection of Olympic medals totals 28, which is a world record in itself—no other athlete has won that many Olympic medals.

In 1956, the Olympics were held in two countries

Australia was the official host of the 1956 Summer Olympics. However, as a country that relies on livestock as one of its main sources of income, Australia has very strict laws about quarantining animals that are brought into the country. This caused a problem for the equestrian events, and so those events were held in Stockholm, Sweden five months prior to the Olympics.

However, this is not the first time this occurred. In 1920, the Summer Olympics were held in both the Netherlands and Belgium due to issues with World War I (WWI).

The only city to host the Olympics three times

London has hosted the Olympics three times: in 1908, 1948, and 2012, and is the only city in the world to do so.

The Paris Olympics of 1900

The very first women athletes to compete in the Olympics took part in the 1900 Paris games. Even when the Olympics were revived in 1894 by Coubertin, only male athletes took part. The very first modern Olympics was held on April 6, 1986.

How would you like to take part in a mountain bike race underwater?

The annual North Carolina Underwater Bike Race is conducted off the

Beaufort Inlet. The races take place where a reef has been created by the sinking of the USS Indra. The cyclists can peddle, push or drag their bikes along the ocean floor to get to the finish. No motorized bikes are allowed though.

TOP SPORTING RECORDS

1. The longest-ever golf putt was 395 feet. It was made by Bret Stanford from the How Ridiculous Club, an Australian YouTube trick shot team. The putt was made in 2017 at the Point Water Golf Club in Australia.

2. The world record holder for performing consecutive push-ups is Japan's Minoru Yoshida. He performed a total of 10,507 push-ups without stopping in 1980.

3. Bill Mosienko from Canada set the record for the fastest hat trick in the National Hockey League when he scored three goals in just 21 seconds. Wow, that is amazing! And did you know that you can watch that amazing feat on YouTube? Just search for Bill Mosienko's hat trick.

4. Ben Smith holds the record for running the greatest number of marathons consecutively. He ran a total of 401 marathons in 401 days! I would have loved to run with him, kids!

The longest-ever boxing match

Can you guess how long this record-breaking match lasted? A whopping 110 rounds which last more than seven hours. The match was in 1893, between Jack Burke and Andy Bowen.

Who won? No one. It was declared "no contest" by the referee who thought enough was enough. Both boxers were exhausted, most of the spectators had fallen asleep, and Andy Bowen ended up with multiple fractures in his hands.

WHAT SPORT DID ABRAHAM LINCOLN PLAY?

Wrestling! That's right, Abe Lincoln was a very good wrestler who rarely lost a match. He boxed for about 10 years during his youth.

Our past president was a very good sportsman in his youth. His achievements in wrestling were recognized in 1992 by the Wrestling Hall of Fame when he was inducted as "Outstanding American" in wrestling.

Quick Sports Quiz

Here's a quick quiz I devised to test your knowledge of sports. Give yourself one point for every correct answer. The answers are on the next page, so no peeking!

1. Backstroke, crawl, and breaststroke are methods in which sport?

2. What does "NBA" stand for?

3. How long is a marathon?

4. What was the very first sport played on the moon?

5. Name the sport for which legend Mohammed Ali was famous.

6. 'Love' is a score in which game?

7. A move was banned in the game of basketball between 1967 and 1976, what was it?

8. Which is the only country that has played in every World Cup football match?

9. Which team has scored the most points in the Super Bowl in NFL history?

10. In which year did women first take part in the Olympics, and what were the sports they participated in?

Sports Quiz—Answers

1. Backstroke, crawl, and breaststroke are methods in which sport?

   Swimming

2. What does "NBA" stand for?

   National Basketball Association

3. How long is a marathon?

   26.2 miles (42.195km)

4. What was the very first sport played on the moon?

   Golf. NASA astronaut Alan Shepard took along some golf clubs and balls when he blasted off to space on February 6, 1971, aboard the Apollo 14. Once on the moon, he played a quick (and the first) game of golf.

5. Name the sport for which legend Mohammed Ali was famous.

   Boxing

6. 'Love' is a score in which game?

   Tennis

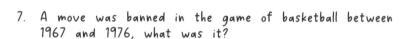

7. A move was banned in the game of basketball between 1967 and 1976, what was it?

   The slam dunk

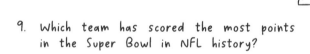

8. Which is the only country that has played in every World Cup football match?

   Brazil

BRAZIL

9. Which team has scored the most points in the Super Bowl in NFL history?

   The San Francisco 49ers when they won Super Bowl XXIX.

10. In which year did women first take part in the Olympics, and what were the sports they participated in?

    In 1900, women entered the Olympics for the first time; 22 women were among the 997 athletes participating, and they competed in tennis, golf, croquet, equestrianism, and sailing.

Chapter 8: Engineering Marvels

 Marvelous designs and mind-boggling structures created by man make our world all the more interesting to explore.

For thousands of years, mankind has been constructing towers, castles, fortresses, shrines, and more that have withstood the test of time.

How awesome are the pyramids of Egypt?

What about the Great Wall of China?

What you see in this picture is the Eiffel Tower in Paris.

As you may recall I was turned into Ronny the Super Dog there. I enjoy visiting the tower and being among the happy tourists wandering around exploring the great monument. Have you been to Paris? You should ask your parents to take you there for your next holiday, maybe we'll bump into each other and share a croissant!

All these structures were designed by skilled engineers and took many years to construct. Engineering marvels are not just limited to buildings; the construction of thousands

of miles of railroads, towers, and cables that connect the entire world, and even man-made beaches are all included. Next, we are going to explore some of the world's most impressive constructions.

Historical Engineering Marvels

The Panama Canal

The Panama Canal was opened in 1914. It is a 51-mile-long channel that connects the Pacific and Atlantic Oceans. International trade received a huge boost once the canal was opened because ships now had a shorter route to get from the Pacific to the Atlantic, or vice-versa.

Fifty-six thousand workers toiled to create the canal, cutting through thick jungle. Sadly, 10% of the workers died while working on the canal due to exhaustion and disease. The amount of soil excavated to create the canal is said to have been enough to cover the entire island of Manhattan.

The Golden Gate Bridge

Opened in 1937, the Golden Gate Bridge was, for the first 27 years, the world's longest suspension bridge. The bridge stretches for 1.7 miles above the channel that connects the Pacific Ocean with the San

Francisco Bay.

Did you know the bridge is actually orange in color even though its name is the 'Golden' Gate Bridge?

The Undersea Channel Tunnel

I have traveled through the channel tunnel from my hometown in France to visit London in England. This is one of the best creations by modern engineers and links the European continent to the island of Britain.

It took six years to build the tunnel, which opened in 1994. It is 31 miles long and stretches across the English Channel connecting the two landmasses. Twenty-three miles of it runs through the sea at 150 feet under the surface to transport cars, buses, cargo vehicles, and even trains. Because of the tunnel, I can get from London to my home in Paris in just two and a half hours. All I have to do is hop on the super-fast Eurostar train. Of course, people have the option of driving along the tunnels, too.

The International Space Station

One of man's greatest achievements, the International Space Station (ISS), is about the size of an American football field. It weighs a mega 925,000 pounds and has enabled scientists to learn a lot about space by living and working there.

ISS orbits Earth every 90 minutes while traveling at a

speed of 17,500 miles per hour. There are many services provided by ISS including helping NASA to learn more about space while aiding its exploration of Mars. Researchers aboard ISS are also looking for cures for diseases.

The Statue of Liberty

The Statue of Liberty was gifted to the US by the French in 1886. The gift was given as an act of friendship and was appreciated. The majestic 151-foot-tall statue was impressive and beautiful—it still is. A French sculptor from Paris, Frederic-Auguste Bartholdi, made the statue's skin from large sheets of copper in France. It was then sent in 200 crates to New York. Did you know the statue is a green color today because of the oxidation of the copper plates?!

Tallest Man-Made Waterfall

Did you know that one of the world's largest man-made waterfalls is in China?

It is not located in a park or tropical forest. Oh no, this humongous waterfall is located in the Liebian International Building in the Guizhou Province.

The waterfall is created by using huge pumps to rotate water stored in giant tanks.

The water is pumped to the top of the building where it falls 121 meters down its side, creating a stunning waterfall.

The Burj Khalifa

This is the tallest building in the world as of 2022. The Burj Khalifa is located in Dubai, a Middle Eastern city renowned for its architectural marvels. Located in Downtown Dubai, the tower is also home to one of the world's tallest mosque observation decks, and even one of the largest fountains in the world.

The Great Wall of China

This is one of the Great Wonders of the World and certainly one of the greatest engineering feats achieved by man. The Great Wall took over 2,000 years to be completed because the wall kept getting extended into different sectors; to protect the Silk Road, it was extended toward the west, and then into the Yumen Pass, which took nearly 400 years.

The best progression the wall made was in the 14th century when China was under the rule of the Ming Dynasty. Bricks and stone were used to make the wall more sturdy because the main purpose of its construction was to protect China from invasions by the Mongolians.

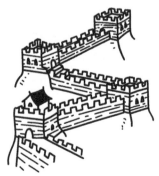

The walls stretch a distance of 13,171 miles and contain watch towers, bridges, and even pagodas. It crosses 15 provinces and is one of China's main attractions.

Have you visited the Great Wall of China?

Conclusion

Okay, kiddos, that's the end of our journey for now, but I promise I've got heaps more facts to share with you. Watch out for my next big book to join me, Ronny the Frenchie, on more adventures around the world.

For now, I want to thank you for being such good students, and I am awarding you with the three-star badge I give to all my followers.

Welcome to the Ronny Fact-Finding Club! You are now an official member. I hope my book has inspired you to learn more about our wonderful planet and to try and make discoveries of your own.

Explore as much as you can. Start with your backyard and the park— you will be surprised by the amazing discoveries you can find there. Insects, plants, critters, and so much more just waiting to be found.

Remember, kids, that knowledge is power. Never stop learning and always believe in yourself. Catch you on my next adventure!

Have a paw-some day!

References

The absence of the concept of zero in Roman numerals system. (n.d.). Roman Numerals https://www.romannumerals.org/blog/the-absence-of-the-concept-of-zero-in-roman-numerals-system-8

Adebowale, T. (2021, August 25). *The best 61 sports facts for kids.* Kidadl. https://kidadl.com/articles/best-sports-facts-for-kids

Afzal, A. (2010, May 9). *What is a baker's dozen and how did the phrase originate?* The Times of India. https://timesofindia.indiatimes.com/what-is-a-bakers-dozen-and-how-did-the-phrase-originate/articleshow/5908384.cms

Alem. (n.d.). *7 weird animal facts that you didn't know.* The Pet Express. https://thepetexpress.co.uk/blog/general-interest/7-weird-animal-facts-that-you-didnt-know/

All About Frogs. (n.d.). Burke Museum. https://www.burkemuseum.org/collections-and-research/biology/herpetology/all-about-amphibians/all-about-frogs

Ancient Egyptian Inventions. (n.d.). https://www.clark-shawnee.k12.oh.us/userfiles/98/Classes/4758/ancient%20egypt%20inventions.pdf?id=11293

Andrews, E. (2020, January 30). *11 things you may not know about Ancient Egypt.* History. https://www.history.com/news/11-things-you-may-not-know-about-ancient-egypt

Apodyterium. (n.d.). PBS. https://www.pbs.org/wgbh/nova/lostempires/roman/apodyterium.html

Ask Smithsonian. (2020, April 1). *Is it true that elephants can't jump?* Smithsonian Tween Tribune. https://www.tweentribune.com/article/tween78/it-true-elephants-cant-jump/

Auckland, G. & Gorst, M. (n.d.). *There is no zero in Roman numerals. Who invented zero, and when?* The Guardian. https://www.theguardian.com/notesandqueries/query/0,5753,-1358,00.html

Bath, G. (2020, August 23). *Tilly Smith was taught about tsunamis in her geography class. What she learnt saved 100 lives.* Mamamia. https://www.mamamia.com.au/tilly-smith-tsunami/

Beasely, J. (2021, August 11). *The 7 wonders of the engineering world.* Institution of Civil Engineers (ICE). https://www.ice.org.uk/news-and-insight/ice-community-blog/august-2021/wonders-of-engineering-world

Best nature videos for kids. (n.d.). Easy Science for Kids. https://easyscienceforkids.com/best-nature-videos-for-kids/

Biancolin, B. (2018, November 26). *25 seriously weird things we can actually buy in Japan's vending machines.* TheTravel. https://www.thetravel.com/weird-things-we-can-actually-buy-in-japans-vending-machines/

Bindschadler, R. (2005, June 27). *Why is the South Pole colder than the North Pole?*

Scientific American. https://www.scientificamerican.com/article/why-is-the-south-pole-col/

Blakemore, E. (2018, November 20). *Turkeys were once worshipped like gods.* History. https://www.history.com/news/turkey-worship-maya

Bond, H. (2021, April 28). *50 best frog puns and jokes that are toad-ally funny.* Kidadl. https://kidadl.com/articles/best-frog-puns-and-jokes-that-are-toad-ally-funny

A brief history of reed pens. Find out how to make your own. (2017, September 1). Paper Stone Blog. https://www.paperstone.co.uk/News/2017/history-reed-pens

BRINK Editorial Staff. (2014, December 30). *More people have cell phones than toilets.* BRINK News. https://www.brinknews.com/more-people-have-cell-phones-than-toilets/

British Museum Blog. (2021, February 26). *Top 10 historical board games.* The British Museum. https://blog.britishmuseum.org/top-10-historical-board-games/

Brnakova, J. (2021, January 22). *12 cool facts about South America for all ages.* Kiwi.com. https://www.kiwi.com/stories/12-cool-facts-south-america-for-all-ages/

Buckley, S. (2022, February). *Fiber will (mostly) dominate broadband in 2022.* Broadband Communities. https://www.bbcmag.com/community-broadband/fiber-will-mostly-dominate-broadband-in-2022

Burke, A. (2022, April 25). *Do dogs sweat? You may be surprised by the answer.* American Kennel Club. https://www.akc.org/expert-advice/health/do-dogs-sweat/

Buzz Staff. (2021, February 16). *Did you know that a pie chart is called "Camembert" in France and "flatbread chart" in China?* News18. https://www.news18.com/news/buzz/did-you-know-that-a-pie-chart-is-called-camembert-in-france-and-flatbread-chart-in-china-3439967.html

Cahn, Lauren. (2022, May 31). *The 18 smartest dog breeds.* Reader's Digest. https://www.rd.com/list/smartest-dog-breeds/

Can certain snails really sleep for 3 years? (2019, July 19). A-Z Pet Vet. https://www.azpetvet.com/can-certain-snails-really-sleep-for-3-years/

Capitol rotunda. (n.d.). Architect of the Capitol. https://www.aoc.gov/explore-capitol-campus/buildings-grounds/capitol-building/rotunda

Carey. (2016, May 4). *Things they do differently in Paraguay.* Our Nomadic Experience. http://ournomadicexperience.com/things-differently-paraguay/

Cell phone facts for kids. (n.d.). Facts Just for Kids. https://www.factsjustforkids.com/technology-facts/cell-phone-facts-for-kids/

Chantel, J. (2022, June 15). *Smartphone history: Looking back (and ahead) at a modern*

marvel. Textedly. https://blog.textedly.
com/smartphone-history-when-were-
smartphones-invented

*Chinese firm to recycle "panda poo" into tissue
paper.* (2017, December 20). BBC News.
https://www.bbc.com/news/42422216

Chirag. (2020, November 12). *Did you know the heart
of a shrimp is in their head?* Chirag's
Blog. https://chiragsoccer.wordpress.
com/2020/11/12/did-you-know-the-
heart-of-a-shrimp-is-in-their-head/

*CH 103—Chapter 7: Chemical reactions in biological
system.* (n.d.). Western Oregon
University. https://wou.edu/chemistry/
courses/online-chemistry-textbooks/
ch103-allied-health-chemistry/ch103-
chapter-6-introduction-to-organic-
chemistry-and-biological-molecules/

Cocoa's history. (n.d.). Cacao México. https://
cacaomexico.org/?page_id=70&lang=en

Culture facts for kids. (2022, April 9). Kiddle. https://
kids.kiddle.co/Culture

Curran, A. (2020, November 16). *Why do airplanes
avoid flying over the Himalayas?* Simple
Flying. https://simpleflying.com/why-
do-airplanes-avoid-flying-over-the-
himalayas/

Darwin's Frog. (2021, February 16). A-Z Animals.
https://a-z-animals.com/animals/
darwins-frog/

Debunking owl myths. (n.d.). International Owl Center.
https://www.internationalowlcenter.org/
mythsandfaq.html

Diakite, P. (2019, July 31). *Here are the most popular
tribes in Africa.* Travel Noire. https://
travelnoire.com/here-are-the-most-
popular-tribes-in-africa

Dickerson, K. (2015, June 3). *Mount Everest isn't
the Earth's tallest mountain.* Business
Insider. https://www.businessinsider.
com/earths-tallest-mountain-is-
hawaii-2015-6

Dobrijevic, D.. (2022, January 21). *How Hot Is the
Sun?* Space.com. https://www.space.
com/17137-how-hot-is-the-sun.html

Dotson, J.D. (2018, November 14). *Definition of
tectonic plates for kids.* Sciencing.
https://sciencing.com/definition-
tectonic-plates-kids-8509085.html

Dousdebes, F. (2016, August 29). *20 fun facts about
the Galapagos Islands.* Metropolitan
Touring. https://www.metropolitan-
touring.com/facts-galapagos/

Do volcanoes occur in the ocean? (2021, February
26). NOAA. https://oceanservice.noaa.
gov/facts/volcanoes.html

Dubey, N. (2021, January 10). *When Steve Jobs
unleashed the iPhone: 10 amazing
facts from the 2007 launch.* The Indian
Express. https://indianexpress.com/
article/technology/mobile-tabs/when-
steve-jobs-unleashed-the-iphone-
10-amazing-facts-from-the-2007-
launch-7140916/

Ducksters. (2022). *Physics for kids: Nuclear energy
and fission.* Ducksters. https://www.
ducksters.com/science/physics/
nuclear_energy_and_fission.php

Duncan, E. & Dally, T. (2021, September 23). *As
autumn approaches here's why we see
more spiders in our houses and why
wasps are desperate for sugar.* The
Conversation. https://theconversation.
com/as-autumn-approaches-heres-
why-we-see-more-spiders-in-our-
houses-and-why-wasps-are-desperate-
for-sugar-167593

Eatner, J. (2014). *Obelus.* A Maths Dictionary for Kids.
http://www.amathsdictionaryforkids.

com/qr/o/obelus.html

Echarri, M. (2021, March 15). *Were the Vikings fashion
trendsetters of the Medieval age?* EL
PAÍS English Edition. https://english.
elpais.com/usa/2021-03-15/were-the-
vikings-fashion-trendsetters-of-the-
medieval-age.html

The Editors of the Encyclopedia Britannica. (n.d.).
Black death key facts. Britannica.
https://www.britannica.com/summary/
Black-Death-Key-Facts

The Editors of Encyclopedia Britannica. (2018b).
*Black Death | Causes, Facts, and
Consequences.* Britannica. https://www.
britannica.com/event/Black-Death

The Editors of Encyclopedia Britannica. (2022, March
25). *Great Barrier Reef | Geography,
Ecology. Threats, & Facts.* Britannica.
https://www.britannica.com/place/
Great-Barrier-Reef

The Editors of Encyclopaedia Britannica. (2019).
Roman Numeral | Chart & Facts.
Britannica. https://www.britannica.com/
topic/Roman-numeral

Egypt Today Staff. (2020, September 27). *How did
Champollion decipher the hieroglyphs
on the Rosetta Stone?* Egypt Today.
https://www.egypttoday.com/
Article/4/92430/How-did-Champollion-
decipher-the-hieroglyphs-on-the-
Rosetta-Stone

85% of plant life is found in the ocean. (2018,
June 10). Did You Know Stuff. http://
didyouknowstuff.com/85-of-plant-life-
is-found-in-the-ocean

Erickson, K. (2022, June 22). *How long is one day on
other planets?* NASA Science Space
Place. https://spaceplace.nasa.gov/
days/en/

Eveleth, R. (2013, May 17). *Two-thirds of the world
still hates lefties.* Smithsonian Magazine.
https://www.smithsonianmag.com/
smart-news/two-thirds-of-the-world-
still-hates-lefties-64727388/

*Fantasmagorie, the world's first fully animated
cartoon, was released on Aug 17, 1908:
Watch it here.* (2017, August 18). India
Today. https://www.indiatoday.in/
education-today/gk-current-affairs/
story/fantasmagorie-first-animated-
film-1030219-2017-08-18

15 facts about the human body! (n.d.). National
Geographic Kids. https://www.
natgeokids.com/uk/discover/science/
general-science/15-facts-about-the-
human-body/

15 things you didn't know about Dr. Livingstone.
(2014, October 26). Sun International.
https://www.suninternational.com/
stories/travel/15-things-you-didnt-
know-about-dr-Livingstone/

Facts & figures. (2022). The Empire State Building.
https://www.esbnyc.com/about/facts-
figures

Ferocious Media. (2019, August 13). *Why left-handed
athletes have the upper hand in one-
on-one sports.* Orthopaedic Specialty
Group, P.C. https://www.osgpc.com/
left-handed-athletes-in-sports/

Finch, R. (2022, January 14). *How many noses does a
slug have?* Pests Banned. https://www.
pestsbanned.com/snails/how-many-
noses-does-a-slug-have/

Finley, K. (2016, April 27). *Hey, Nokia isn't just
a company that used to make
phones.* Wired. https://www.wired.
com/2016/04/hey-nokia-isnt-just-
company-used-make-phones/

Fire whirl. (n.d.). SKYbrary. https://skybrary.aero/

articles/fire-whirl

The first circumnavigation of the globe. (2020, February 26). Library of Congress. https://www.loc.gov/rr/hispanic/portam/first.html

Fischer, S. (2012, November 14). *What lives in your belly button? Study finds "rain forest" of species.* National Geographic. https://www.nationalgeographic.com/science/article/121114-belly-button-bacteria-science-health-dunn

Fodor's Editor. (2010, October 27). *10 things to know when visiting Greece.* Fodor's Travel Guide. https://www.fodors.com/news/customs-and-eti-5-4139

Fourtané, S. (2018, September 18). *Galapagos islands: Muse of Darwin's theory of evolution.* Interesting Engineering. https://interestingengineering.com/galapagos-islands-muse-of-darwins-theory-of-evolution

Frietmuseum. (n.d.). Friet Museum. http://frietmuseum.be/en/home-en/

Frost, N. (2017, August 11). *Did mooncakes help the Chinese overthrow the Mongols?* Atlas Obscura. https://www.atlasobscura.com/articles/mooncakes-china-mongols-manchu-metaphor-uprising

Gallo, N. (2021, October 29). *10 fun facts about Antarctica.* Aurora Expeditions. https://www.aurora-expeditions.com/blog/10-fun-facts-about-antarctica/

George, A. (2018, April 11). *The sad, sad story of Laika, the space dog, and her one-way trip into orbit.* Smithsonian Magazine. https://www.smithsonianmag.com/smithsonian-institution/sad-story-laika-space-dog-and-her-one-way-trip-orbit-1-180968728/

Giddens, S. (2020, October 13). *Flatulence: Everything you wanted to know about farting.* Houston Methodist. https://www.houstonmethodist.org/blog/articles/2020/oct/flatulence-everything-you-wanted-to-know-about-farting/

Glass, A. (2007, October 30). *Rosa Parks mourned at Capitol, Oct. 30, 2005.* Politico. https://www.politico.com/story/2017/10/30/rosa-parks-honored-at-us-capitol-oct-30-2005-244294

Goodwins, R. (2006, November 17). *Muscle means "little mouse" in Latin...* ZDNet. https://www.zdnet.com/article/muscle-means-little-mouse-in-latin/

Grabianowski, E. (n.d.). *How many skin cells do you shed every day?* HowStuffWorks. https://health.howstuffworks.com/skin-care/information/anatomy/shed-skin-cells.htm

The Greek gods: Full list and background. (2020, October 31). Greek Travel Tellers. https://greektraveltellers.com/blog/the-greek-gods

Griffin, E.C., Dorst, J.P. & Minkel, C.W. (n.d.). *South America.* Britannica. https://www.britannica.com/place/South-America

Griffiths, J. (2022, February 15). *How long is the Great Wall of China and why was it built?* The Sun. https://www.thesun.co.uk/travel/2711342/great-wall-china/

Guajardo, M, Meister, C., Bunning, M., Warren, L., & Dekevich, C. (n.d.). *Strawberries.* Food Source Information. https://fsi.colostate.edu/strawberries/

Guess which country has built the world's tallest man-made waterfall? (2018, August 1). South China Morning Post. https://www.scmp.com/magazines/style/news-trends/article/2157574/guess-which-country-has-built-worlds-tallest-man-made

Harper, W.L. (2012, May). *Isaac Newton's scientific method: turning data into evidence about gravity and cosmology.* University Press Scholarship Online. https://oxford.universitypressscholarship.com/view/10.1093/acprof:oso/9780199570409.001.0001/acprof-9780199570409

Hayes, D. (2017, May 31). *Average U.S. household now has 7 screens, report finds.* Fierce Video. https://www.fiercevideo.com/cable/average-u-s-household-now-has-seven-screens-reportlinker-finds

Hickey, W. (2012, July 22). *20 mathematicians who changed the world.* Business Insider. https://www.businessinsider.com/important-mathematicians-modern-world-2012-7#james-maxwell-the-first-color-photographer-2

History of key—who invented keys? (2022). History of Keys. http://www.historyofkeys.com/keys-history/history-of-keys/

History.com Editors. (2021, October 12). *Rosie the Riveter.* History. https://www.history.com/topics/world-war-ii/rosie-the-riveter

History.com Editors. (2021, November 30). *Ford's assembly line starts rolling.* History. https://www.history.com/this-day-in-history/fords-assembly-line-starts-rolling

History of the UN. (2015). United Nations. https://www.un.org/un70/en/content/history/index.html

Hofmeyr, A. (2018, December 30). *African culture, tribes & traditions (and our top pick of cultural tours in Africa).* African Budget Safaris. https://www.africanbudgetsafaris.com/blog/african-tribes-african-culture-and-african-traditions/

Holi. (n.d.). Society for the Confluence of Festivals in India. https://www.holifestival.org

Holi 2021 date and time: Why two different Holi dates in India. (2021, March 18). India Today. https://www.indiatoday.in/information/story/holi-2021-date-and-time-why-two-different-holi-dates-in-india-1780777-2021-03-18

Hot spots. (n.d.). National Geographic Society. https://www.nationalgeographic.org/encyclopedia/hot-spots/

Hottest countries in the world 2022. (n.d.). World Population Review. https://worldpopulationreview.com/country-rankings/hottest-countries-in-the-world

How big is the magma chamber under Yellowstone? (n.d.). US Geological Survey. https://www.usgs.gov/faqs/how-big-magma-chamber-under-yellowstone

How does an underwater volcano form? (n.d.). Deutsche Welle. https://www.dw.com/en/how-does-an-underwater-volcano-form/a-60453856

How fast can neurons transmit through your body for the nervous system to function? (n.d.). UCSB ScienceLine. http://scienceline.ucsb.edu/getkey.php?key=5607

How hot is lightning? (n.d.). National Weather Service. https://www.weather.gov/safety/lightning-temperature

How many satellites are there in space? (2022, February 22). Surveying News. https://surveyinggroup.com/how-many-satellites-are-there-in-space-2022/

Howard, B. C. (2014, January 30). *Stunning Electric-Blue Flames Erupt From Volcanoes*. National Geographic. https://www.nationalgeographic.com/science/article/140130-kawah-ijen-blue-flame-volcanoes-sulfur-indonesia-pictures

The human brain. (2022, June 24). Rehabilitation Info Portal. http://www.rehabchicago.org/the-human-brain/

Human body trivia. (n.d.). Fizzics Education. https://www.fizzicseducation.com.au/trivia/science-trivia-on-the-human-body/

Hunt, A. (2020, January 30). *20 intriguing facts about New Zealand that you probably didn't know: illustrated*. Silver Fern Holidays. https://www.silverfernholidays.com/blog/20-intriguing-facts-new-zealand/

Hurst, H.E. & Smith, C.G. (2019). *Nile River*. Britannica. https://www.britannica.com/place/Nile-River

Is a "jiffy" a real unit of measurement? (with picture). (2022, May 18). WiseGEEK. https://www.wisegeek.com/is-a-jiffy-a-real-unit-of-measurement.htm

James, R. (n.d.). *Why can't helicopters land on Mount Everest—Yet?* Pilot Teacher. https://pilotteacher.com/why-cant-helicopters-land-on-mount-everest-yet/

Joe. (n.d.). *How many sheep are in New Zealand*. RaisingSheep.net. https://www.raisingsheep.net/how-many-sheep-are-in-new-zealand

Jozuka, E. (2016, September 22). *Aboriginal Australians are Earth's oldest civilization: DNA study*. CNN. https://edition.cnn.com/2016/09/22/asia/indigenous-australians-earths-oldest-civilization/index.html

J. Robert Oppenheimer. (n.d.). Atomic Heritage Foundation. https://www.atomicheritage.org/profile/j-robert-oppenheimer

July 20, 1969: one giant leap for mankind. (2019, July 20). NASA. https://www.nasa.gov/mission_pages/apollo/apollo11.html

Jung, A., Jones, M., & Taubenfeld, E. (2022, June 13). *30 fun facts about dogs*. Reader's Digest. https://www.rd.com/list/dog-facts-you-didnt-know/

Juraschka, R. (2021, September 23). *101 silly math jokes and puns to make students laugh like crazy*. Prodigy. https://www.prodigygame.com/main-en/blog/math-jokes/

Kaddour, N. (2020, May 20). *African tribal make-up: what's behind the face paint?* Al Arabiya News. https://english.alarabiya.net/life-style/fashion-and-beauty/2016/11/26/African-tribal-make-up-What-s-behind-the-face-paint

Kangaroos. (2019, January 14). *Australia's beloved kangaroos are now controversial pests*. National Geographic. https://www.nationalgeographic.com/magazine/article/australia-kangaroo-beloved-symbol-becomes-pest

Kelly, R. (2020, January). *Best left-handed athletes of all time*. Stadium Talk. https://www.stadiumtalk.com/s/best-left-handed-athletes-49fb6ddc95a043c3

Kidadl Team. (2022, May 3). *60+ great stem quotes for science-loving kids*. Kidadl. https://kidadl.com/quotes/great-stem-quotes-for-science-loving-kids

Kim, S.E. (2021, December 20). *Cultivating the world's largest, stinkiest flower is no small task*. National Geographic. https://www.nationalgeographic.com/environment/article/cultivating-the-worlds-largest-stinkiest-flower-is-no-small-task

Klein, A. (2021, August 30). *7 strange German superstitions and cultural beliefs*. LearnOutLive. https://learnoutlive.com/german-superstitions-cultural-beliefs/

Klein, C. (n.d.). *10 world engineering marvels*. History. https://www.history.com/news/10-world-engineering-marvels

Kolirin, L. (2022, January 26). *Meet 190-year-old Jonathan, the world's oldest-ever tortoise*. CNN. https://edition.cnn.com/travel/article/oldest-tortoise-jonathan-scli-intl-scn/index.html

Kõljalg, S., Mändar, R., Sõber, T., Rööp, T., & Mändar, R. (2017). *High level bacterial contamination of secondary school students' mobile phones*. National Library of Medicine. https://www.ncbi.nlm.nih.gov/pmc/articles/PMC5466825/

Kronvall, A. (n.d.). *Facts about Greenland*. Nordic Co-operation. https://www.norden.org/en/information/facts-about-greenland

Landslides and mudslides. (2018, January 12). Centers for Disease Control and Prevention. https://www.cdc.gov/disasters/landslides.html

Langley, L. (2016, October 29). *A frog whose babies pop out of its back and more freaky animals*. National Geographic. https://www.nationalgeographic.com/culture/article/animals-halloween-bats-scary-freaky

Lăpuşneanu, D. (n.d.). *87 Australian slang terms to help you speak like a true Aussie*. Mondly. https://www.mondly.com/blog/2020/05/14/87-australian-slang-terms-speak-aussie/

Lavrov, I. (2021, July 27). *Mozilla Firefox logo design—history, meaning and evolution*. Turbologo Blog. https://turbologo.com/articles/mozilla-firefox-logo/

Leatherback turtle facts. (2019). World Wildlife Fund. https://www.worldwildlife.org/species/leatherback-turtle

Littlechild, C. (2021, June 10). *The strange underwear requirement baseball umpires have to follow*. Grunge. https://www.grunge.com/433937/the-strange-underwear-requirement-baseball-umpires-have-to-follow/

Lohnes, K. & Sommerville, D. (n.d.). *Battle of Thermopylae*. Britannica. https://www.britannica.com/event/Battle-of-Thermopylae-Greek-history-480-BC

Manfred, T. (2014, June 12). *The real reason Americans call it "soccer" is all England's fault*. Business Insider. https://www.businessinsider.com/why-americans-call-it-soccer-2014-6

Mark, J. J. (2013, November 14). *Alexander the Great*. World History Encyclopedia. https://www.worldhistory.org/Alexander_the_Great/

McLoughlin, C. (n.d.). *Sports trivia questions for kids*. SignUp Genius. https://www.signupgenius.com/sports/kids-trivia-questions.cfm

McMahon, S. (2017, July 13). *The ultimate guide to Olympic snowboarding at PyeongChang 2018*. Onboard Magazine. https://onboardmag.com/news/snowboarding-events/ultimate-guide-olympic-snowboarding-pyeongchang-2018.html#ABzTv8XUZ9z71sHj97

Migiro, G. (2018, July 19). *The major religions of Asia*. WorldAtlas. https://www.worldatlas.com/articles/the-major-religions-of-asia.html

Mitsopoulou, T. (n.d.). *The color blue for repelling*

evil. Greece Travel. https://www.greecetravel.com/archaeology/mitsopoulou/blue.html

Morocco. (n.d.). UNESCO World Heritage Centre. https://whc.unesco.org/en/statesparties/ma

Murray, B. (n.d.). *Were the Neanderthals smarter than we are?* Fortinberry Murray. https://www.fortinberrymurray.com/todays-research/were-the-neanderthals-smarter-than-we-are

Muzzaffar, M. (2021, July 27). *Watch: Chinese city of Dunhuang swallowed up by gigantic wall of sand.* The Independent. https://www.independent.co.uk/climate-change/china-dunhuang-sandstorm-desert-video-b1891141.html

NAACP. (2016). NAACP. https://naacp.org

Newman, D. (2022, February 12). *20 coldest countries in the world [2022 Coldest Country].* What's Danny Doing? https://www.whatsdannydoing.com/blog/coldest-countries-in-the-world

North America Facts. (2022, May 11). Facts.net. https://facts.net/north-america-facts/

Norway offers tuition-free quality education. (n.d.). University of Bergen. https://www.uib.no/en/education/109728/norway-offers-tuition-free-quality-education-it-2018-2

Noses and ears continue to grow as we age. (n.d.). The Dr. Oz Show. https://www.drozshow.com/noses-ears-grow-with-age

Nowak, C. (2018, February 12). *The world's longest place name has 85 letters — see if you can pronounce it.* Business Insider. https://www.businessinsider.com/the-worlds-longest-place-name-has-85-letters-see-if-you-can-pronounce-it-2018-2

Oct 4, 1957 CE: USSR launches Sputnik. (n.d.). National Geographic Society. https://www.nationalgeographic.org/thisday/oct4/ussr-launches-sputnik/

O'Leary, M.B. & Iandoli, E. (2013, May 30). *How the turtle got its shell—clues revealed by fossils.* Elsevier Connect. https://www.elsevier.com/connect/how-the-turtle-got-its-shell-revealed-by-fossils

Orca killer whale vs. great white shark: who wins in a fight? (n.d.). Nature Noon. https://naturenoon.com/orca-killer-whale-vs-great-white-shark/

Our top 10 sporting facts to satisfy your sports trivia appetite. (2016, August 17). Challenge Trophies. https://www.challengetrophies.co.uk/blog/top-10-sporting-facts-sports-trivia/

Patel, P. (2022, April 20). *When and why did we start using math symbols?* Science ABC. https://www.scienceabc.com/pure-sciences/start-using-math-symbols.html

Payne, L. (n.d.). *What animals cannot walk backwards?* Pets on Mom. https://animals.mom.com/animals-cannot-walk-backwards-3794.html

Pele's curse: why you should never take lava rocks from Hawaii. (n.d.). Hawaii Guide. https://www.hawaii-guide.com/why-you-should-never-take-lava-rocks-from-hawaii

'Pinocchio effect' confirmed: when you lie, your nose temperature rises. (2012, December 3). ScienceDaily. https://www.sciencedaily.com/releases/2012/12/121203081834.htm

Plants. (n.d.). British Antarctic Survey. https://www.bas.ac.uk/about/antarctica/wildlife/plants/

Poison dart frog. (n.d.). National Geographic Kids. https://kids.nationalgeographic.com/animals/amphibians/facts/poison-dart-frog

Prostak, S. (2012, August 1). *Study finds shark teeth as hard as ours.* Science News. http://www.sci-news.com/biology/article00499.html

Qin, A. & Chien, A. C. (2022, April 7). *When you hear Beethoven, it's time to take out the trash (and mingle).* The New York Times. https://www.nytimes.com/2022/02/08/world/asia/taiwan-waste-management-beethoven.html

Culture in South America. (n.d.). The South America Specialists. https://www.thesouthamericaspecialists.com/node/471

Kiwi facts. (n.d.). Rainbow Springs Nature Park. https://www.rainbowsprings.co.nz/kiwi-conservation/kiwi-facts/

Top ten awesome facts about frogs. (n.d.). Earth Rangers. https://www.earthrangers.com/top-10/top-ten-awesome-facts-about-frogs/

Rogozinski, D. (2020, November). *7 world history facts that will amaze your kids.* Study.com. https://study.com/blog/7-world-history-facts-that-will-amaze-your-kids.html

Rosa Parks. (2022). NAACP. https://naacp.org/find-resources/history-explained/civil-rights-leaders/rosa-parks

The Rosetta Stone. (n.d.). Khan Academy. https://www.khanacademy.org/humanities/ancient-art-civilizations/egypt-art/x7e914f5b:late-period-ptolemaic-and-roman-periods/a/the-rosetta-stone

Saiidi, U. (2018, February 21). *Australia's banknotes may be the most advanced in the world.* CNBC. https://www.cnbc.com/2018/02/21/australian-banknotes-one-of-the-most-advanced-in-the-world.html

SaltWire Network. (2017, October 2). *Spell numbers until you find the letter A.* SaltWire. https://www.saltwire.com/cape-breton/opinion/spell-numbers-until-you-find-the-letter-a-20263/

The Samburu Tribe of Kenya and East Africa. (2022). Siyabona Africa. https://www.siyabona.com/samburu-tribe-kenya-culture.html

Sengupta, S. (2022, March 8). *Holi 2022: 5 traditional foods to enjoy on Holi.* NDTV Food. https://food.ndtv.com/food-drinks/holi-2019-5-traditional-foods-to-enjoy-on-holi-2001236

Sengupta, T. (2021, November 23). *NASA posts pic of a blue sunset on the Red Planet. Seen viral share yet?* Hindustan Times. https://www.hindustantimes.com/trending/nasa-posts-pic-of-a-blue-sunset-on-the-red-planet-seen-viral-share-yet-101637655239320.html

7 other reasons to visit Africa. (n.d.). World Expeditions. https://worldexpeditions.com/Blog/reasons-to-visit-africa

Short history of sundials. (2019, April 27). European Association for Astronomy Education. https://eaae-astronomy.org/find-a-sundial/short-history-of-sundials

Shvili, J. (2021, March 11). *How many countries are there in Asia?* WorldAtlas. https://www.worldatlas.com/articles/how-many-countries-are-in-asia.html

Silly trivia. (2015). Signal Station Pizza. http://www.signalstationpizza.com/trivia.html

Sissons, C. (2020, June 7). *How much blood is in the*

human body?. Medical News Today. https://www.medicalnewstoday.com/articles/321122

Small, M. F. (2007, July 6). *Mummy reveals Egyptian queen was fat, balding and bearded*. Live Science. https://www.livescience.com/7336-mummy-reveals-egyptian-queen-fat-balding-bearded.html

Smarter than you think: Renowned canine researcher puts dogs' intelligence on par with 2-year-old human. (2009). American Psychological Association. https://www.apa.org/news/press/releases/2009/08/dogs-think

Songkran festival: Everything you need to know. (2015, December 9). Hostelworld Blog. https://www.hostelworld.com/blog/songkran-everything-you-need-to-know/

South America map. (n.d.). InfoPlease. https://www.infoplease.com/atlas/south-america

Spector, D. (2019, July 25). *Why extreme heat turns train tracks into spaghetti.* Business Insider. https://www.businessinsider.com/why-train-tracks-buckle-in-extreme-heat-2013-7

Staff Writer. (2020, April 13). *What is the longest recorded flight of a chicken?* Reference.com. https://www.reference.com/pets-animals/longest-recorded-flight-chicken-5abd0ed8b465850f

The story behind the Mozilla Firefox logo. (2019, June 14). Free Logo Design. https://www.freelogodesign.org/blog/2019/06/14/the-story-behind-the-mozilla-firefox-logo

Strege, J. (2022, February 3). *How astronaut Alan Shepard brought golf to space 51 years ago with his celebrated "Moon shot."* Golf Digest. https://www.golfdigest.com/story/alan-sheperd-apollo-14-moon-shot-50th-anniversary-history

Team Mighty. (2022, May 8). *20 rare and weird facts about World War 2.* We Are the Mighty. https://www.wearethemighty.com/lists/21-rare-and-weird-facts-about-world-war-2/

Technology and invention. (2022). Britannica Kids. https://kids.britannica.com/kids/article/Technology-and-Invention/353296

10 facts about Ancient Egypt. (n.d.). National Geographic Kids. https://www.natgeokids.com/uk/discover/history/egypt/ten-facts-about-ancient-egypt/

10 interesting facts about the dead sea. (2022, June 14). On the Go Tours Blog. https://www.onthegotours.com/blog/2019/05/facts-about-the-dead-sea/

Ten largest American Indian tribes. (2017, February 28). Infoplease. https://www.infoplease.com/us/society-culture/race/ten-largest-american-indian-tribes

The 10 most venomous animals in the world! (2020, October 30). AZ Animals. https://a-z-animals.com/blog/the-10-most-venomous-animals-on-earth/

Top 10 facts about the Mayans! (n.d.). Fun Kids. https://www.funkidslive.com/learn/top-10-facts/top-10-facts-about-the-mayans/

Torgan, C. (2014, March 31). *Humans can identify more than 1 trillion smells.* National Institutes of Health. https://www.nih.gov/news-events/nih-research-matters/humans-can-identify-more-1-trillion-smells

The Trajan's markets and Trajan the Roman Emperor. (2022). Italy Travels. https://www.museumsrome.com/en/our-blog-on-rome/the-trajan-s-markets-and-trajan-the-roman-emperor

20 cool facts about maths. (n.d.). Maths-whizz. https://www.whizz.com/blog/20-cool-facts-maths/

Visitthecapitol.gov. (n.d.). https://www.visitthecapitol.gov/sites/default/files/images/Podcast/EP9/EP9-RosaParksReflections-MASTER-Mixdown.cleanCL2.pdf

Wei-Haas, M. (2018, January 15). *Volcanoes, explained.* National Geographic. https://www.nationalgeographic.com/environment/article/volcanoes

What food do Thai people eat at Songkran? (n.d.). Meat and Supply Co. https://www.meatandsupplyco.com/what-food-do-thai-people-eat-at-songkran/

What is an earthquake and what causes them to happen?. (2013). U.S. Geological Survey. https://www.usgs.gov/faqs/what-earthquake-and-what-causes-them-happen

What is the difference between "magma" and "lava"? (n.d.). U.S. Geological Survey. https://www.usgs.gov/faqs/what-difference-between-magma-and-lava

What is the highest point on Earth as measured from Earth's center? (2022, January 19). NOAA. https://oceanservice.noaa.gov/facts/highestpoint.html

What is the longest putt ever made in golf history, certified by Guinness? (2017, April 5). Golf News Net. https://thegolfnewsnet.com/golfnewsnetteam/2017/04/05/longest-putt-ever-made-golf-history-guinness-world-record-101932/

When were potatoes used as currency? (n.d.). G. Visser & Sons. https://gvisser.ca/fun-fact/when-were-potatoes-used-as-currency

Why do airplanes avoid flying over Pacific Ocean and Mt Everest? (2020, February 10). India Today. https://www.indiatoday.in/lifestyle/travel/story/why-do-airplanes-avoid-flying-over-pacific-ocean-and-mt-everest-1643604-2020-02-05

Why mosquitoes are the deadliest animal in the world. (2022). Terminix Triad. https://www.terminix-triad.com/about/our-blog/why-mosquitoes-are-deadliest-animal-world

Wilkinson, F. (2019, January 22). *Want to climb Mount Everest? Here's what you need to know.* National Geographic. https://www.nationalgeographic.com/adventure/article/climbing-mount-everest-1

Your guide to the world. (n.d.). Nations Online. Www.nationsonline.org. https://www.nationsonline.org/oneworld/africa.htm

Your mouth produces about one litre of saliva each day! (2021, March 7). Croucher Science Week. https://crouchersscienceweek.hk/everyday-science/saliva/